Heart and Darkness

Scary Adventures and the Evolution of Disney's Dark Rides

Shawn Patrick Farrell

Theme Park Press
The Happiest Books on Earth
www.ThemeParkPress.com

Theme Park Press publishes its books in a variety of print and electronic formats. Some content that appears in one format may not appear in another.

Editor: Bob McLain
Layout: Artisanal Text

ISBN 978-1-68390-096-2
Printed in the United States of America

Theme Park Press | www.ThemeParkPress.com
Address queries to bob@themeparkpress.com

CONTENTS

Introduction

When recounting an experience in the Reptile House of the London Zoological Gardens, Charles Darwin, the British naturalist and geologist, and arguably history's most revered voice on the subject of evolution, wrote in his ground-breaking book *The Expression of Emotions in Man and Animals*:

> My will and reason were powerless against the imagination of a danger which had never been experienced.

Pressing his face close to the glass barrier and determined to remain perfectly at ease, each time the venomous puff adder he was observing lunged forward in an attempt to attack him, Darwin could not help but jump back out of fear.

While he had never personally experienced the bite of a deadly snake, he knew instinctively how to react, recoiling as quickly as possible despite the safety of the glass. Darwin continued:

> Terror causes the body to tremble. Skin becomes pale, sweat breaks out and the hair bristles. The secretions of the alimentary canal and of the kidneys are increased and they are involuntarily voided... The breathing is hurried. The heart beats quickly, wildly and violently. The surface seems bloodless and the strength of the muscles soon fails... The mental faculties are much disturbed... Utter prostration soon follows, and even fainting...

Nearly a century and a half later, while we live in a dramatically different world, the symptoms of terror as described by Charles Darwin have not changed. The instinctive reaction to thrills, fear, and terror have remained decidedly the same.

Yet even as renewed threats of global nuclear catastrophe surface; even as society continues to be ravaged by plagues ranging from AIDS to Zika; even as science has long dismissed many of the supernatural phenomena still believed in Darwin's day, humanity relishes the opportunity to mingle with the macabre. At the dawn of the 21st century, fear is more boundless than ever before: from an endless supply of comic books, music, and movies, to video games, toys, and even breakfast cereals, our taste for fear cannot be confined to a single genre. While nowadays we have come to fear the menace of the sinister Count Chocula more for his sugar content than the more nefarious designs a vampire may have on our well-being, our fascination lingers. Can you imagine a child anywhere on this earth unfamiliar with vampires, or given the current obsession, clueless about zombies?

In his introduction to H.P. Lovecraft's *Supernatural Horror in Literature*, which examines the horror genre in British and American literature over the course of two centuries, E.F. Bleiler states:

> The oldest and strongest emotion of mankind is fear, and the oldest and strongest kind of fear is fear of the unknown.

This instinctive reaction to fear, coupled with our cultural fascination with being scared and just as importantly the curious habit of anticipation, which allows us through a shared experience enriched by mass media, whether it may be an earthquake, plane crash, or deadly chase, to understand and feel a similar response to any such stimuli, without actually having experienced it, has been of tremendous benefit to those tasked with the design of amusement park rides, who have been trained to anticipate how these fears manifest within us and how best to exploit them for maximum thrills. For if we know what *might* happen as we board any ride meant to scare us out of our wits, we are that much closer to believing that it *will*.

Leaping forward from Darwin and Lovecraft to Walt Disney finds us in the realm of another legendary historical figure. When the cartoon maker turned theme park impresario opened Disneyland in 1955, it included three attractions based on some of his most beloved properties: Snow White's Scary Adventures, Mr. Toad's Wild Ride, and Peter Pan's Flight. These are stories that had been familiar to Disney audiences for some time, and longer still to those familiar with their celebrated source material. Some years later, after virtually re-inventing the concept of the theme park, Disney's innovations continued, as park guests first became acquainted with the Pirates of the Caribbean and wandered through the creepy corridors of the Haunted Mansion.

By the time Walt and his Imagineers began to dream up Disneyland, the concept of the dark ride had become quite familiar to amusement park guests. Understood generally as indoor experiences that used a minimal amount of lighting to gradually reveal spooky scenes with music and sound effects, the earliest incarnations of dark rides predated Disneyland by several decades. Far different from traditional amusements such as carousels, merry-go-rounds, and Ferris wheels, these rides played on our delight in being scared and had been of interest to thrill seekers for some time.

The Disney difference, and its core appeal as evidenced by the enduring popularity of these attractions, rests not entirely in their ability to scare audiences outright, as is the common aim of more low-brow amusement park rides, but in a careful and balanced mix of the fun and the fearful, and in what we know with what we may not, along with the resultant thrills and delights provided by that uncertainty.

For over 60 years, it has been that careful balance, coupled with a flair for innovation that has left Disney unique among its peers and has enabled Disney to find the heart within the darkness. As riders journey into the dimness of the unknown, they draw comfort in that whatever frights may await them, there is always going to be light at the end.

CHAPTER ONE

Engineering Terror

The precise date marking the invention of the dark ride has been lost to time and has long been disputed; however, its earliest precursors are undeniable, the first of which were known as scenic railways that began to take shape in the decades following the American Civil War. While the technology behind roller coasters was still in its infancy, the crudest scenic railways inherited some of their inspiration from the 17th century Russian "mountains" that were built into the icy hills near St. Petersburg, Russia.

Some years later, American ingenuity led to many early patents intended to enhance this type of experience. The first such patent, concerning improvements to inclined railways, was granted to John G. Taylor of Baltimore, Maryland, in 1872. The earliest of these crude structures were entirely outdoors and the focus of the ride was on its climactic drop, until LaMarcus Thompson arrived in Coney Island in the spring of 1884 to begin the construction of his innovative switchback railroad.

Thompson leased a lot on W. 10th Street and Surf Avenue and eventually as many as 10 passengers at a time would careen at the less-than-intoxicating speed of 6 miles per hour over metal tracks set into a wooden frame, creating an immediate hit for passengers intent on a more thrilling adventure. Thompson's attraction had the added benefit of providing riders with a scenic tour of the beach, or as scenic as possible given the ride's 20-second duration. People would wait in line for as long as three hours for the experience, paying a nickel per ride.

Skilled in the art of self-promotion, "Thompson boasted to eager Brooklyn and Manhattan newspaper reporters that he conceived his ride while watching happy riders screaming in delight on his friend's circular ride in Louisiana," according to Jeffrey Stanton in "Early Roller Coasters: 1870-1886." But he had loftier ambitions, soon crafting a ride that offered park visitors a more engaging view than a loop would provide. The publicity he gained made his ride even more popular, with offers to purchase his invention pouring in from all over the world. The first sale was to the owners of the Euclid Beach resort outside of Cleveland, Ohio.

Thompson's ride owed a considerable debt to John G. Taylor's earlier innovations, but it was his highly publicized effort that quickly spawned imitations near and far. Multiple competitors began vying for their share of that nickel fare even as Thompson awaited the approval of his patent. Cheaply made copies began sprouting up in and around Coney Island and elsewhere within a matter of weeks.

Of all his would-be imitators, it was the arrival of Philip Hinkle not one year later that nearly sent Thompson off the rails. Hailing from San Francisco, California, Hinkle, who was in the elevator business, envisioned an improved but still primitive circular scenic railway using a winch-and-pulley mechanism to lift passengers up a hill. He was awarded a patent for a steam-powered hoist that pulled cars loaded with riders up an incline, while fasteners gripped the underside of the car, pulling it along. This approach was not too far removed from current technology, although it lacks decades of advances in safety features.

Hill's innovations led to a faster ride, but also gave passengers the chance to sit facing forward, allowing them to look in the direction of the coaster's movement. Faced with this intrusion on his livelihood, along with that of his lesser imitators, LaMarcus Thompson spent the remaining years prior to the turn of the century focused less on speed and drops and continued the promotion of sightseeing as the key component of his designs, in the process being granted 30 additional patents.

In 1886, with the assistance of a Philadelphia inventor named James A. Griffith, another roller-coaster pioneer, Thompson began developing what would eventually be remembered as the definitive scenic railway in Atlantic City,

New Jersey, when it opened the following year. This latest design incorporated a steam-powered lift, a single continuous track, and carefully designed scenery with blinking lights to accentuate the views. At specific points throughout the ride, floodlights would reveal Biblical scenes.

The excitement over Thompson's latest work, coupled with his savvy marketing, led to his design of 20 additional scenic railways and another two dozen in Europe before the turn of the century. Brandon Kwaitek, in "The Dark Ride," observed that "by 1888, Thompson had built nearly fifty gravity rides in the United States and Europe." Much like Walt Disney several decades later, Thompson's dependence on his craft gave him the financial incentive to continue innovating, but his design in Atlantic City is considered to be the first modern dark ride, for despite its long stretch of outdoor track, it also employed dark tunnels with special effects and brief narrative episodes. The ride's cars would trigger a series of switches that revealed the illuminated scenes or play music or sound effects.

In fact, some suggest that Thompson's meticulously executed pattern of thrills and illusions helped prepare an eager public for the eventual magic of the motion picture and so created a relationship between dramatic storytelling and the concept of the dark ride that Walt Disney would later revolutionize.

Much later, in Europe, a new attraction was introduced as the first ride to be called a ghost train, making its debut at Blackpool Pleasure Beach in Blackpool, Lancashire, England, in 1930. Designed by Joseph Emberton, this imported novelty was meant to capitalize on the British public's lack of familiarity with the popular pretzel rides already common in the United States. Called simply the Ghost Train, it was named after a popular play of the time known for its dazzling special effects. In "A Short History of Ghost Train Rides," Lawrence Daz wrote: "The unique selling factor was to brand these cars as trains and to garishly adorn the advertising banners outside with suggestions of the scares and thrills within." Rebuilt in 1936, and having since gone through numerous revamps, it remains a popular Blackpool attraction today, and notably also shares real estate with Valhalla, considered the largest indoor dark ride in the world.

Though public spectacles featuring ghostly projections had been popular since the 1800s, not until Blackpool Pleasure Beach, already a popular diversion for guests for many years, combined the elements of the supernatural, carnival freak shows, effects, illusions, and spectacle in its ghost train, were so many of these ideas mixed together in a single attraction.

As amusement parks and their most enjoyable rides flourished in America after their earliest successes in Coney Island and Atlantic City, enterprising developers of more modest means sought inexpensive but equally enjoyable alternatives, which gave birth to the pretzel ride.

Leon Cassidy and Marvin Rempfer patented their single-rail dark ride in 1928, when they, as struggling owners of the Tumbling Dam Amusement Park in Bridgeton, New Jersey, hoped to build a water ride. but found it cost prohibitive. Instead, they conceived of a waterless version of the then-common old mill ride that would run on a single electric rail. The ride took its name after a guest commented that he felt as if he'd been twisted into a pretzel due to its many turns. When the ride opened, it met with a great deal of success and their newly formed Pretzel Amusement Company began offering their patented ride design nationwide at the much more affordable rate of $1200. Initially, their standard design weighed roughly 9 tons and featured 5 cars that would travel over 350 feet of track over the course of a 90-second ride. Unloaded on site by huge moving vans, the pieces were assembled and customized to the specifications of park owners.

As reported by ridemad.com, in "Early Dark Ride History in a Nutshell":

> The Pretzel Ride took the amusement business by storm. Routinely outgrossing all other rides on the midway, Pretzels were rapidly being installed in nearly every fun park in the nation, and foreign countries were also asking for them.

The portability and flexible nature of the pretzel ride made it an ideal option for the more itinerant park owners who wanted inexpensive versatility. To further advertise their brand, a heavy, oversized pretzel was placed on the front of each car, which had the added benefit of weighing the cars down and preventing them from flipping backwards. In the late 1950s, the Pretzel Amusement Company expanded its offerings to include a two-story option, where the cars were raised to the second level by a lift chain. Nearly doubling the weight of the single-story option, this version still took only five hours to assemble.

In "The Historical Development of Themed Space," Sam Coons observed:

> The Pretzel's flexible format and low costs made it a versatile option for park owners, and William Cassidy would estimate that 1,200 to 1,500 were produced before his company ceased production in 1979."

Spared the effort and expense of ride design, park owners instead focused on theming and created attractions with themes as diverse as the Haunted House, Winter Wonderland, Orient Express, Paris After Dark, and Treasure Island.

Camden Park, in Huntington, West Virginia, can boast of offering one of the few remaining haunted house pretzel rides. The exact date of its opening is unknown, but it is believed they began operation with a single-story version and later expanded to the larger model in the 1960s.

First to notice the appeal of pretzel rides across the Atlantic, Joseph Emberton and the owners of Blackpool Pleasure Beach were quick to capitalize on the thrill of fear, using the colorful banners outside of the ride to hint suggestively at the terrors that awaited within.

As was the case with each new, and more importantly profitable, innovation in amusement park rides, ghost trains soon caught on elsewhere in the United Kingdom, as each provided their own variation on Blackpool's twists, turns, and sudden drops. The two-person cars embarked suddenly on their effects-laden journey past monsters and ghosts punctuated by eerie noises or a flash of light, reminiscent of Charles Darwin's reaction in the Reptile House of the London Zoological Gardens.

These rides became so successful and competition for the attention of thrillseekers so intense that Emberton returned to Blackpool to enhance his standard setting ride still further.

Beyond the addition of iconic characters from the horror and supernatural realms of popular culture that were added in the 1940s, he designed a new façade for the ride and a new, two-level roller coaster built within, again upping the ante for competitors in the field, among them Pleasure Beach in Great Yarmouth and Pleasureland in Southport.

While carnival barkers and advertisements used every trick in the book to draw attention to their ghost train and better sell the frightful experience that no doubt awaited their patrons, it was unfortunately the very innovation of the ghost train that ultimately led to its demise. The primary appeal to amusement park owners was that a ride be inexpensive, simple to run and maintain, and in the case of traveling fairs, easy to transport to a new location. As profitable as ghost trains were, they became increasingly massive in scale with their many high altitude drops, twists, and turns, and therefore far too complex to easily dismantle.

Still, there are survivors from this bygone era, including the original Ghost Train at Blackpool and others that have carried its concepts forward.

Old Mills and New Ideas
Waterways to Wonder in the Dark

Still decades before we would follow Mr. Toad on his wild ride, and a malevolent, ghostly bride pleaded with riders to "hurry back," anxious thrill-seekers boarded another far more leisurely mode of conveyance to sate their interest in the dark and mysterious. Dating back to the late 19th century, passengers rode aboard small boats through dark passages carved into tunnels and caves on a type of amusement park attraction best known as an old mill.

The first of these old mills is said to have been created by London inventor Arthur Pickard, who in 1891 fashioned an experience where small, two-passenger boats with motorized propellers made their way through a twisting waterway, touring a representation of the ride's namesake, the Canals of Venice.

Meanwhile in America, long before the railways that enthralled a young Walt Disney began their dominance of American commerce and travel, transit via waterways both natural and man-made was the norm. In the early part of the 19th century, water-powered sawmills were prevalent throughout many parts of the country. Rapidly advancing technology during the Industrial Revolution introduced steam power, which led to a proliferation of steam-powered railways and mills. As a result of this new technology, many of the water-powered sawmills were closed or abandoned, with the towns that had sprung up during more prosperous days often following suit.

As these mills, houses, shops, and buildings were deserted and left to ruin, rumors spread about some of them being haunted. Opportunistic entrepreneurs who wisely thought of capitalizing on these rumors and the public's interest in the supernatural built replicas of these abandoned structures as paid attractions, offering guests a combination of nostalgia mixed with fear and excitement.

One of the earliest examples of this subset of the American entrepreneurial spirit was Kennywood Amusement Park in Pittsburgh, Pennsylvania, which began operation in 1898 as a small trolley park and is still welcoming guests today. Much like Disneyland's humble origins, the park began as a grove of trees on farmland owned by Anthony Kenny. Since the American Civil War, local residents made use of this spot, with its picturesque view of the Monongahela River, to relax and enjoy picnics.

In 1898, the Monongahela Street Railways Company, eager to increase weekend fare revenue courtesy of these local residents, leased Kenny's land to create a trolley park at the end of their rail line. Their ambitions matured, and a carousel, casino, and dance hall were added before the turn of the century, with the Old Mill opening in 1901. It afforded trolley park guests the opportunity to safely experience re-creations of places that, while more than familiar to anyone of the era, were traditionally off-limits to all but experienced professionals.

Another early leap forward in the development of dark rides opened in Coney Island's Sea Lion Park in 1902. Designed

by George W. Schofield, this old mill also used the theme of
a run-down Pennsylvania mill, but in this incarnation, there
were dark tunnels and spooky scenery featuring a variety of
monsters and ghouls meant to scare unsuspecting riders. In
their book *The American Amusement Park*, Dale Samuelson
and Wendy Yegoiants wrote: "Drawing upon the grist mill as
inspiration, a powered waterwheel at the entrance would add
theming, as well as provide the current necessary to propel
the boats." Like Pickard's Canals of Venice, boats that resembled gondolas would continuously float through these stylized
waterways, but with the added element of theming.

Schofield's design resonated spectacularly with American
audiences reeling from the rapid modernization of their lives.
Their excited nostalgia for the recent and curiously haunted
past led to the popularity and proliferation of old mills in
amusement parks throughout the country. His design replaced
the propellers used by Thompson with a large waterwheel to
maintain a steady flow of water and conveniently support the
grist mill theme of the attraction, but the greatest enhancement was the tunnels that riders traveled through to witness
the spectacular scenes.

Fittingly, in their tamest and most innocent incarnation,
these old mills were often called a tunnel of love. Very much
a product of this more austere period, two passengers would
depart for a romantic cruise into darkness where they might,
albeit briefly, escape prying eyes and enjoy some privacy,
enjoying a socially acceptable excuse for intimacy that would
have been frowned on in the light of day. Ride developers soon
seized on the opportunity to exploit this interest and many
rides were re-themed, resulting in the tunnel of love quickly
becoming commonplace in amusement parks as a frequent
retreat for those interested in passionate seclusion. Braver
couples might opt for a spookier alternative, with frightening
spooks and scenes peppered throughout to provide a similarly
convenient opportunity for physical contact, as frightened
passengers leapt into the comforting arms of their sweetheart.

Whatever the purpose of their voyage, be it scary, romantic, or even a trip through history, riders never had to worry
about veering off course, as old mills were the first type of

amusement ride where passengers sat in a vehicle—which in this case was a boat following a narrow water course. Along the way, unless the riders were otherwise engaged, they'd encounter various scenes or figures, typically mannequins made of wax that depicted various characters appropriate to the theme of the ride.

Old mills were expensive to build and maintain because they required a tunnel with some manner of waterway and a wooden water wheel constantly in motion to push water through the canal. Park staff had to inspect the waterway often for leaks and tend to costly repairs in the off-season. Surviving old mills have long since converted to concrete waterways that are chemically treated to prevent leakage.

Their frequent and expensive maintenance meant that only the most expensive parks could support old-mill attractions. Perhaps that is one of the reasons that after less than a decade of operation, the trolley company that owned Kennywood Park no longer wanted to run it, opting in 1906 to lease it.

That may have been a prudent move on their part, for while the park is still in operation today and is doing a great deal of business based on nostalgia for this simpler time, as the years passed and more prudish customs gave way to a greater range of socially acceptable opportunities for unmarried couples to engage in physical contact, old mills began to fade in popularity. Many were torn down to make way for new developments; others were re-themed for children or repurposed as more exciting attractions.

Earliest among these repurposed alternatives were spruced-up variations on the old mills known as river caves. These rides take their name from the common theming of underground caves with styrofoam rock formations jutting this way and that, and presenting detailed displays depicting scenes of history and fantasy from around the world. Riders would still meander slowly through the man-made canals and twisty caves and tunnels on a current powered by a paddle wheel, but with the stigma of paramours in close quarters having lessened, more emphasis was put on spectacle, as new and more modern visual effects, props, and lighting were added to the scenes.

Through the mid-20th century, river-cave rides were increasingly common throughout Great Britain and the United States, whether they were man-made to meet the interest of the public, or repurposed versions of old mills. Often offering passengers a chance to be educated as well as entertained, these attractions would also gradually lessen in popularity, as park guests craved bigger and better thrills, and they have since become exceptionally rare. One of the most popular examples of river caves still open today can be found approximately 80 miles south of Indianapolis, Indiana. The Bluespring Caverns is an hour-long boat ride where the focus is on the natural wonders seen along the way, ranging from an underground river to the bats, fish, and other wildlife lurking throughout its dimly lit corridors.

Still another variation on old mills that saw increasing popularity in the 1920s and 1930s and has since evolved into many beloved rides still in operation today are mill chutes. These rides, geared even more toward thrill seekers, feature roller-coaster-like drops at the end.

One such ride was in operation for over 40 years at Hersheypark in Derry Township, Pennsylvania. Founded in 1906 by the famous American confectioner Milton S. Hershey, Hershey Park, as it was then known, replaced an existing pool in 1929, and the valuable park real estate was designated for the Mill Chute. Re-themed as the Lost River in 1963 following renovations that were required due to its state of disrepair, it remained open until destroyed by a hurricane in 1972.

Mill chutes were mainly manufactured throughout the 1920s and 1930s, while old mills were mainly manufactured in the late 19th century and into the 1930s. Though old mills do feature drops, they are not nearly as steep as the climactic drop on a mill chute.

The mill chute is the precursor to the modern-day log flume. An even earlier version, called a shoot-the-chutes, opened in Brooklyn's Coney Island in 1895. Though designed more for the splash factor and absent the prelude of a journey through a darkened cavern, these ride spawned countless imitators their heyday in the 1920s and 1930s, until the public's fascination with them began to fade in the aftermath of World War II and many began to vanish, along with their accompanying amusement parks.

Always seeking to build on what came before, amusement park innovators often repurpose the best elements of past attractions into something newer and more exciting. The Philadelphia Toboggan Company was one of the first to combine the old mill and shoot-the-chutes. Mill chutes typically featured the same darkened grottos and narrow passageways as old mills, but similar to their descendants, including Splash Mountain, boats were drawn to the top of an incline and then released, giving passengers the added thrill of a final, large drop just after they once again glimpse the light of day and just before being soaked at the ride's end, as their boat rapidly skids over a pool.

To Infinity and Beyond
Or, to the Moon and Back

Even as the concepts of amusement parks, and later dark rides, were still relatively new to audiences in search of the next best thing, their methods of conveyance were based on paths already traveled. For most, travel by train, and certainly water, was old hat, and it was the sights, sounds, and thrills offered by these attractions that kept them coming back for more.

Yet there was one final frontier for humanity to conquer, and the opportunity to do just that and still make it home by dinner debuted in 1901 to attendees of the Buffalo Pan American Exposition, who were bold enough to go on A Trip to the Moon.

Even without the grandeur and tremendous hype generated by the Expo, this attraction quickly achieved the E-ticket status of its day, bolstered by technology and investment typical of the Disney attractions that the world would first witness more than half a century later.

Much like Walt Disney, who would one day envision his own Disneyland as an opportunity for guests to temporarily escape the mundane drudgery of everyday life, Frederic Thompson hoped to develop a new level of ride that would

offer a similar reprieve from the ordinary. Already a successful architect and designer of park buildings throughout the
United States, his intent was to craft a new form of amusement that would exploit modern technology, machinery, and
imagination, and introduce the world to not only a new form
of themed entertainment, but also essentially showcase the
first flight simulator.

Also anticipating the Disney approach to ride development,
Thompson drew inspiration from many of the popular interests
and stories of his day, settling on an innovative mix of science
fiction and fantasy. While it might seem quaint to modern
audiences, a trip to the moon was wholly new for the America
of 1901, and when Thompson added modern technologies of
the age, like electric light, the result was a smash success.

Banking on that potential appeal, Thompson spent nearly
$85,000 (equivalent to over $2 million today) to design and
build his attraction. Central to the experience was a fanciful
30-passenger spacecraft that resembled a boat with enormous
wings made of red canvas. Suspended overhead by steel cables,
which gave just enough leeway for the craft to swing about in
the air, it had wings controlled by a pulley system, and multiple lights and sounds to round out the exterior.

Every thirty minutes, and for the price of fifty cents, guests
(some of whom may have read Jules Verne's 1865 novel *From
the Earth to the Moon*) could now explore this strange new
world. Thompson's attraction anticipated several other elements that would later be typical of many of Disney's theme
park rides, including a pre-show where those about to take
flight gathered in an auditorium where an attendant representing the "Aerial Navigation Company" would deliver a short
safety message and other information about their pending
journey. Guests would then board their craft, dubbed *Luna*,
and begin their voyage, all of which was contained within
a 40,000-square foot show building.

To enhance the illusion, a series of painted backdrops cycled
past the spacecraft, depicting the ship's launch, travel over
Niagara Falls, through a wall of clouds, and then onward
among the stars, with hidden fans simulating the wind generated by their movement, until finally arriving on the moon

after surviving a perilous electrical storm. Woody Register, in his book *The Kid of Coney Island*, wrote:

> Thompson produced the apparent passage across time and space with an array of clever scenic tricks. The floor beneath the ship was painted to represent the distant ground below, so passengers had the sense that they already were high in the air when they boarded. Passengers entered at one end of the ship, where the scenery depicted an aerial view of the fair, and once the flight ended, exited at the opposite end, where the scenery was that of the principality of the Man in the Moon. Once the flight began, the orchestrated manipulation of scenic screens, which surrounded the ship and were painted to represent clouds, Earth and the Moon, prompted the sensation of rising, forward, and descending movement.

When their journey was over, passengers disembarked and found themselves in an elaborate lunar environment, where they were greeted by a race of alien "Selenites."

Guided by their new alien friends, they made their way through a maze of mineral wonders, stalactites, and other rock formations to the City of the Moon. Scattered throughout the city, they could find a gift shop, sample green cheese, and pass their time exploring other novel attractions. For the show's grand finale, guests made their way to the palace of the Man in the Moon, where they were treated to a dazzling spectacle of lights and dancing fountains, before a less-than-exhilarating exit down a rope ladder.

Maintaining such an ambitious exhibit was no easy task and took nearly 250 employees. But for Thompson, it was an out-of-this-world success, as he would go on to recoup four times his initial investment during the first summer of operation, as more than 400,000 Expo guests boarded his spaceship, among them President William McKinley and Thomas Edison.

It's possible, given the massive success and global attention given to A Trip to the Moon, that French filmmaker George Melies read of it and adapted elements of the attraction for his classic 1902 film of the same name, which does share many similarities to Thompson's ride. In fact, the ride was so successful that when the exposition closed, he moved his attraction from Buffalo to Coney Island, where it would remain, eventually made the centerpiece of Luna Park, for the next 40 years. Register observed:

> Anyone who later embarked on Disneyland's 1955 fantasy Rocket to the Moon or rode E.T.'s flying bicycle at the Universal Studios Orlando theme park experienced a sensation that Thompson brought to market in 1901.

Tragically, business and personal problems followed Thompson's success with this major attraction, and like Walt Disney, he died before his wildest dreams had been realized, at the age of 46. Still, his utilization of story elements, technology, grand showmanship, and exceptional craftsmanship remains even today a blueprint for equally aspirational designers.

CHAPTER TWO

A Trick of the Brain

One of humankind's greatest and most enduring traits is our compulsion to create. Initially, on witnessing the paintings of animals drawn in the caves of Lascaux, France, archaeologists marveled at the artistry of their design, as they had previously not thought early humans capable of such creative expression.

When the caves were first discovered in 1940, those at the scene also uncovered over 100 stone lamps that had long ago been fueled by animal fat. Unfortunately, as it for so long had been understood that prehistoric people used fire merely for cooking and warmth, no one thought at the time to note the location of the lamps spread throughout the site. Had the archaeologists been more conscious of how light would impact the development of early humans, or how the presence or absence of light would alter their perception of the paintings, continued analysis by today's experts would be far better informed. It is only recently that that impact on their perception is beginning to be understood in Lascaux and similar caves that have been found since then.

No doubt the artists responsible for the paintings used fire to see inside the caves, but many now feel that the flickering flames and the position of the lamps may have been vital to the stories they were trying to tell. Nearly 2,000 figures are depicted within the caves, mixing land animals, birds in flight, people, and curious signs and symbols.

Echoing the refrain of "no flash pictures, please" that has been familiar to guests of Disney theme parks around the world for decades, the curator of the Lascaux caves, Jean-Michel Geneste, once remarked that "when you light the whole cave, it is very stupid because you kill the staging." Making matters worse for casual observers and even the more distant, genuine enthusiasts, most have only ever witnessed the paintings in evenly lit and closely cropped photographs, which removes the paintings from their narrative and deadens the colors witnessed by those who would have seen them under the intended conditions.

Geneste continued, "It is very important: the presence of the darkness, the spot of yellow light, and inside it one, two, three animals, no more. That's a tool in narrative structure." The light from one of their lamps would illuminate a single part of a story, much like a chapter reveals only a portion of a book.

The balance of light and dark frames the story for the observer, just as it would almost 20,000 years later for those traveling through Disneyland's Haunted Mansion. In that context, it is quite easy to fathom an observer moving throughout the caves, holding a lamp to gradually illuminate the story being told with every step they take.

Students of art would also note the relative size of the various figures depicted. If the intent was merely to render an animal artistically, the artist would have likely painted a single creature, such as one of the many horses that cover the cave walls, much larger. If, instead, the intent was to depict many animals connected by a narrative, such as a depiction of a hunting party or a herd of bulls, they would have to be much smaller.

Furthermore, the flickering, unsteady light that would have been used by the Paleolithic men and women who viewed these caves would also create the illusion of life and movement. Our eyes undergo a physiological shift when we move in and out of darkness. Light bounces off of the objects in our view and different objects reflect different degrees of light. Light entering our eyes is collected by our retina, then processed by our brain to fashion whatever it is we are looking at. Light is a crucial component of this process—as you would notice how much more difficult it would be to read this page in darkness.

The balance of light is of considerable importance when looking at any artistic rendering, as with a lesser amount of light, colors fade and shadows blend confusingly with the object depicted. Our ability to focus is also dramatically reduced. The impact of this physiological condition on early humans who were observing these caves might have been as if a bull, rendered in paint with multiple legs, in optimal lighting conditions would have appeared as if it were charging forward, in animated motion, like a crude but strikingly effective Zoetrope or the motion of a child's flipbook as the pages are rapidly turned.

To create an understandable story required incredibly complex planning and a precise integration of the storyteller's intent, lighting, and the materials used to create a narrative arc. Lascaux features attempts at techniques such as forced perspective and the successive placement of related images (the legs of a charging bull) to create a sense of motion, both of which would eventually become key tricks of the trade in the Walt Disney animation studios and elsewhere.

These techniques are by no means unique to Lascaux. Predating the Lascaux paintings by as much as 10,000 years, art uncovered within the Chauvet Cave in southern France in 1994 shows similarly rendered animals, including lions, bison, and a wooly mammoth, many of which appear to be in motion, possibly depicting a story of lions stalking their prey. Could these ancient caves and the artwork that they had for so long hidden have been the first steps taken by our species toward cinematic expression?

While it may be premature to retroactively recommend the undeniably skilled artists behind these cave paintings an award for their achievements in cinematography, the combination of narrative and controlled and dynamic motion and the presence or absence of the light that they used would most certainly play an eventual role in the development of the dark ride.

Those of us well-versed in the history of Disneyland know that Walt Disney first conceived of his namesake park while seated on a bench, watching his two young daughters ride the merry-go-round in Los Angeles' Griffith Park. His frequent visits to the park, which he himself found boring, despite the delight of his children, would eventually inspire him to conceive of a much larger and more refined space that entire families could enjoy together.

Walt's exact thought process in the design of Disneyland as he visited Griffith Park with his children week after week will remain a mystery. But by the time he would bring his children to enjoy the rides, he was already an accomplished visual storyteller and his understanding of cinematic technique, combined with his rapidly growing roster of artists and designers, would soon be unparalleled in the industry.

Imagineering Darkness
The Disneyfication of Dark Rides

Walt Disney's interest in grand-scale amusements took root long before those Saturdays spent with his daughters Diane and Sharon in Griffith Park. His father, Elias, had been a construction laborer for the 1893 World's Columbian Exposition in Chicago, and he no doubt delighted Walt and his other young children with stories of its majesty and wonder. Later, Walt would go on to create a Mickey Mouse short to promote the 1939 New York World's Fair and would speak with considerable enthusiasm of his visits to the Golden Gate International Exposition in San Francisco that same year.

As his own good fortune began to multiply in the wake of the tremendous success of his first full-length animated motion picture, *Snow White and the Seven Dwarfs*, Walt immersed himself in the details and design of his new animation studio in Burbank, California, and at one point, as a sign of the pride he took in its completion and the efforts of his studio staff, even considered offering public tours. But he found the idea of studio tours, especially of an animation lot where employees spent most of their time drawing and painting, exceedingly dull. Still, the legions of fans of his cast of animated characters were relentless in their requests to see where Mickey, Minnie, and the rest of his stable of talent called home, and Walt Disney was rarely one to disappoint his fans.

As far back as 1940, Walt had thought of creating scaled displays of his animated characters in their cartoon environments on a plot of land close to the studio, so that potential visitors could see more than just artists bent over their desks.

This idea eventually gave way to others that involved a touring production, dubbed "Disneylandia," that would feature animated miniature scenes of America's idyllic past and visit department stores across the country.

As the years passed and Disney dealt with the frustrations of a studio mogul that would include an embarrassing strike by the studio's artists and reduced revenue as a result of World War II, his plans for a themed location continued and would coalesce in a 1948 studio memo that featured detailed descriptions of Main Street, U.S.A. and Frontierland. Some four years later, he submitted a plan for an amusement park to the city of Burbank for approval, now including early hints at what would become Tomorrowland and Fantasyland, and by 1953 he began working with the Stanford Research Institute to find the optimal location for his park.

The opening of Disneyland in Anaheim, California two years later was a turning point, not just for the continued fortunes of Walt Disney and his empire, but for the entire amusement park industry. Integrating his vision of what a theme park should be with an even earlier version of the Frank Capra idyll, his keen insight into the nostalgia for fantasy and futurism, and a healthy mix of corporate paternalism, Disney reintroduced a world that had grown weary or even fearful of amusement parks (which for some time had been viewed as dirty, dull, and unsafe places for the evolving standards of modern society) to the concept of escapism. He said:

> I don't want the public to see the world they live in while they're in the park. I want them to feel they're in another world.

Walt believed that every element of his theme park should contribute to telling its story, with guests walking through and experiencing a living show. Though his vision for what would guests would encounter once they passed through the gates of his magic kingdom, or "the art of the show," would evolve in the years after its opening, certain key elements from its original prospectus remain intact to this day:

> Disneyland will be the essence of America as we know it
> ... the nostalgia of the past with exciting glimpses into

the future. ... It will be a place for people to find happiness and knowledge.

In a secure, pristine, and welcoming environment, guests of all ages could enjoy the Disney universe they had come to know through decades of cinema, print media, and television. When Disneyland opened in the summer of 1955, it was as close as possible to Walt's idealization of what an amusement park should be like. From its single point of entry and hub-and-spoke design, to the spotless nature of the park to the appearance and professionalism of its employees, he had a hand in everything, understanding that what the park represented would be a reflection of him. Of course this oversight extended to the park's attractions, three of which were dark rides on opening day.

Years later, following the extraordinary early success of Disneyland, in a 1958 assessment of "The Disney Secret," *The New York Times* surmised that:

> In the theatre the vital ingredient is not realism, but a blending of the real with the imaginary. The entertainer invites the audience to meet him halfway. This is what has been successfully achieved at Disneyland.

Despite all of his accomplishments and the many public accolades received throughout his storied career, perhaps Walt Disney's most significant contributions to entertainment and to the the realms of yesterday, tomorrow and fantasy that would inhabit his parks for decades to come were his gifts as a storyteller and his ability to not only groom the remarkable talent that populated his studio, but to continue to inspire them, even long after his passing.

The three dark rides to instantly enthrall the public on the opening of Disneyland were all based on animated features produced by the studio. Snow White's Scary Adventures, Mr. Toad's Wild Ride, and Peter Pan's Flight raised the standard of dark rides to a new level by introducing a clear and exciting narrative, due largely to the fact that many of those Walt drafted to work on the rides came straight from his story and animation division. These "Imagineers," as they would eventually come to be known, were chosen by Disney with the understanding that they would approach the design of the new dark rides just as they would any film they had worked on. In other words, he knew that they would bring to the table a strong understanding of plot and the importance of showmanship.

In mapping out the attractions, these early Imagineers made use of a number of the Disney studio's pioneering filmmaking techniques, including storyboards and special effects, along with ensuring their attractions included a clear and compelling beginning, middle, and end. Furthermore, riders were not merely to be witnesses to the dramatic elements being presented, as if they were watching the story of a play unfold, but subject to full immersion in the story, as if they were as active in its telling as the cinematic heroes they had come to enjoy, sometimes going so far as to even replace them in the action. But not always: though guests would come face to face with the Seven Dwarfs, the Wicked Queen and any number of forest creatures, those boarding Snow White's Scary Adventures would not witness its titular heroine after they passed the loading track until finally seeing her in the hopeful embrace of her beloved prince.

While Snow White's absence from the story was confusing to some, Disney's approach would become the industry standard in short order, with park guests often assuming the role of the story's protagonist to heighten their immersion. Walt sensed correctly that by casting dark ride passengers in this role, they would feel the same fears, thrills, delights, and relief experienced by their favorite characters.

Beyond serving as a remedy to the displeasure he felt as a parent to his young daughters when visiting Griffith Park, where he found himself not only bored, but uneasy with the park's lack of cleanliness and safety, Walt clearly saw Disneyland and its attractions as another way to engage with his audiences. Most amusement parks, in fact, were like the Warner Bros. cartoons of the late 1940s—noisy, chaotic, bombastic, subversive. One was made to feel that the social rules didn't apply there, that one was entirely free, as Neil Gabler observed in *Walt Disney: The Triumph of the American Imagination*, his biography of Walt. However, like the Disney animated films, over which Walt would personally labor so as to be certain they appealed to each generation and talked down to no one, Walt's passion for bringing the two-dimensional world of his cinematic creations to vivid three-dimensional life in his theme park was clearly a labor of love, ensuring guest satisfaction and comfort.

That same methodology would be ingrained in the Imagineers; it largely would be through their efforts that these dark rides and their surroundings would be rendered so immersive and convincing. Not only would guests feel safe and welcome within Walt's kingdom, they would experience things that they could connect with and respond to on an *emotional* level.

This approach to developing dark rides and many other attractions at the Disney theme parks has remained remarkably unchanged in the decades since Disneyland's opening. The purpose of dark rides is to enable a rider's feeling of escapism by producing a compelling narrative. This was not often the case for earlier rides, such as old mills, which engaged their passengers with thrills, or with mill chutes which heightened their exhilaration with climactic drops, or with the tunnel of love, which offered the potential of illicit romance.

As the world's first truly interconnected theme park, Disneyland aimed to temporarily separate its visitors from their mundane reality and that intent manifested at all levels, from Walt's early goal of giving children the opportunity to meet and mingle with beloved characters like Mickey, Minnie, and Donald Duck and his insistence that cast members from one land within the park never be seen in another, to the design of the dark rides and other attractions.

How he accomplished this is best understood with a look at "Mickey's Ten Commandments," as told to former head of Imagineering, Marty Sklar:

- *Know your audience.* Identify the prime audience for your attraction or show before you begin design.

- *Wear your guest's shoes.* Insist that your team members experience your creation just the way guests do it.

- *Organize the flow of people and ideas.* Make sure there is a logic and sequence in your stories, and in the way guests experience them.

- *Create a wienie (visual magnet).* Create visual "targets" that lead visitors clearly and logically through your facility.

- *Communicate with visual literacy.* Make good use of all the non-verbal ways of communication—color, shape, form, texture.

- *Avoid overload—create turn-ons.* Resist the temptation to overload your audience with too much information and too many objects.

- *Tell one story at a time.* Stick to the storyline; good stories are clear, logical, and consistent.

- *Avoid contradictions—maintain identity.* Details in design or content that contradict one another confuse an audience about your story or the time period it takes place in.

- *For every ounce of treatment, provide a ton of treat.* In our business, Walt Disney said you can educate people—but don't tell them you're doing it! Make it fun!

- *Keep it up (maintain it).* In a Disney park or resort everything must work! Poor maintenance is poor show!

While some are more directly applicable to the development of dark rides than others, each of these directives can be applied to crafting and maintaining a clear and visual narrative and may be interpreted just as easily for filmmaking as theme park and ride design, as they all have the aim of of maximizing the audience's enjoyment of their product, and as such, show the importance of these attractions in enhancing the Disney brand as both a means of entertainment and as works of art.

Defining Darkness
Exactly What Makes a Dark Ride Dark?

Exactly what is a dark ride? Of course, with the near global popularity of the most enduring examples found in Disney theme parks, most everyone is familiar with the term, but not everyone agrees with its meaning. Before proceeding any further, it would serve us well to state firmly what a dark ride is, as the remaining focus of this text will center on how the

Disney Company adopted, modified, and exploited this type of attraction for its theme parks.

In his 1952 book *The Outdoor Amusement Industry: From Earliest Times to the Present*, William F. Mangels describes the dark ride as follows:

> Greatly popular at some resorts are the attractions known as Dark Rides. In these, passenger-carrying vehicles, which may be boats, cars, or small trains, pass through dark tunnels or closed-in passages at a very slow speed. Along the way, surprise scenes such as mechanical ghosts, flirting devils, and similar devices pop up to scare or amuse the slowly passing riders. These devices bear various names. The well-known Tunnel of Love is typical.

While old mills, chutes, scenic railways, and ghost trains all included elements of the Disney dark rides that would follow in the decades to come, from the rudimentary technology of their design and showmanship of their promotion to their scattered attempts at theming, few of these early examples came close to the cohesiveness of the Disney model, and a mere three years later, Mangels' once fitting definition would be in need of considerable revision.

Disney animator and set designer Claude Coats explained how Disneyland's earliest dark rides aimed to distance themselves from the cheap thrills of tunnels of love and carnival spook houses and instead distill the essence of their popular stories into spirited three-minute attractions:

> At that time, most of the little scare rides (at other parks) had very little mood or storytelling qualities. Ken Anderson's storyboards had shown that Peter Pan or Snow White could be told in, not quite a story, but at least a mood that gave the feeling of that story and gave you more than you had if you just went through and saw little scary things.

As we would learn from even their earliest offerings, the Disney dark ride features four key characteristics: physical movement over a track, waterway, or other method, primarily through an enclosed space; a sense of immersion enhanced by scenery, animatronic or stationary figures, and music, narration, and sound effects; the manipulation of light to frame perspective or enhance special effects; and a narrative arc. Disney rides are not dark for their complete absence of light, nor are they excessively dark in terms of content and tone. This definition is flexible enough to fittingly apply to Disney attractions from Anaheim's Snow White's Scary Adventures to Shanghai's Pirates of the Caribbean: Battle for the Sunken Treasure.

Excluded from the definition are those attractions such as roller coasters and motion simulators that simply take place in the dark, like Space Mountain and Star Tours: The Adventures Continue, or thrill rides that may have moments in the dark and no small measure of theming, but lack any sustained narrative element, such as Toy Story Midway Mania, Twilight Zone Tower of Terror, Expedition Everest, and TRON Lightcycle Power Run. For these attractions, the emphasis is more on speed or thrills.

According to Michael Valentino, principal show lighting designer at Walt Disney Imagineering, the main function of show lighting is to help tell the story:

> So we start out with identifying the need. How can we design lighting that creates the mood and feeling of the ride's story? First we look at concept art to get a sense of the overall feeling of what the creative team wants. Next, we brainstorm on ideas on how best to reveal the drama in each scene with just the right lighting.

To visualize the scenes, Imagineers will sometimes map out the attractions with scale models, moving lights around the scenes to get the best sense of what the lighting will do in the fully realized show. Often in a dark ride, the limited lighting must appear to be sourced from whatever direction the viewer is experiencing the scene, which can sometimes present challenges for the Imagineers, who are determined to present their story as realistically as possible, even in a fantasy environment. We can also see the Imagineers' use of color in lighting in various dark rides to further convey certain feelings and emotions in the short amount of time guests view each scene. The flashes of red in the Indiana Jones Adventure suggest the heat of fire and lava and the dangers each present as guests move deeper into the Temple of the Forbidden Eye, and the cold blues and purples of the Haunted Mansion psychologically hint at the icy specter of death.

What guests hear as they progress through the dimly lit corridors of the Haunted Mansion or prepare to do battle against Emperor Zurg plays as crucial a part as light in the storytelling of the Disney dark ride. Sound begins to play a role in the narrative as soon as guest enter the land where an attraction is located. Guests are acclimated to the ride experience gradually and by the time they have boarded their ride vehicle and set off on their journey, they become more and more immersed in the narrative, whether it is the goings-on behind closed doors in the seedy streets and alleys of Toontown, or what they hear off in the distance as passengers set sail into the bayou for a swashbuckling pirate adventure.

"As you continue the experience, the soundscape twists and turns right along with the story," said Joe Herrington, principal media designer at Walt Disney Imagineering, and often makes use of particular elements to punctuate a story point. Speakers may be placed in the ride vehicles, or throughout the attraction at different distances and heights, to create as realistic an experience as possible.

New technologies and renovations of existing rides might allow for the types of attractions listed above that are not considered dark rides to become them by adding the missing component. Disney's Imagineers have always made extraordinary efforts at theming even rides such as roller coasters, where the emphasis is on thrills, so if the attraction's story elements or the manipulation of light were modified, some might more accurately be considered traditional Disney dark rides.

The format of the true Disney dark ride owes its roots to Walt Disney and the early studio work of his animators, as without fail, these rides mirror the narrative structure of a film, in that they each feature a collection of scenes or episodes meant to guide passengers through a fully plotted narrative with a beginning, middle, and end. When combined with special effects wizardry, immersive sound, propulsive musical accompaniment, inviting narration, and the careful manipulation of light where the darkness is used to the designer's advantage, they result in the ride format that Disney all but mastered with even its earliest attempts. As the Imagineers put it,"The match of media and story is a crucial step that blends technology and artistry, engineering and environment." Even as long-standing dark rides and perennial favorites are renovated to include the latest technologies and effects, it is done in service of enhancing the narrative and further immersing riders within that fantasy environment.

Yet, according to Jeff Kurrti and Bruce Gordon, in *The Art of the Walt Disney World Resort*:

> Walt Disney and his creative heirs are often superficially lumped into the category of "fantasy," and too often in a negative way, with a meaning of an unsophisticated lack of reality, a silly insincerity, or a juvenile lack of factual astuteness.

However, the Disney depiction of fantasy is less about the depiction of cliché symbols than it is about how the stories told through their films, and in turn their attractions, have continued to endure for decades. While common archetypes of princesses, wicked queens, and sinister villains may recur in their storytelling, the qualities they have come to represent are exceedingly more important to Disney's longevity and appeal: bravery, wonder, love, hope, imagination, and trust. If a theme park attraction can inspire any of those same feelings in its guests, then it has unquestionably succeeded.

CHAPTER THREE

The Genesis of the Disney Dark Ride

The dawn of the Industrial Age led many more ambitious men and women of the time to revisit the relationship between humanity and mechanization. A nostalgia for that ingenuity, specifically in its American incarnation, was central not only to the theming of Walt Disney's initial foray into the theme park industry, but to the pursuits of the talented men and women who would bring his vision to life through the creation of that park's many ambitious and ground-breaking attractions.

The boundless ambition of its leader, combined with the efforts of his Imagineers, led to Disneyland being the first fully realized commingling of space and narrative and perhaps nowhere has this immersion been better realized than in the park's many storied dark rides.

Opening as Walt's original Magic Kingdom on July 17, 1955, Disneyland served to not only revitalize the amusement park industry with its elaborate theming and attention to detail, it created an entirely new definition for dark ride attractions. Having celebrated its diamond anniversary just prior to the publication of this book, Disneyland has been delighting park goers for generations. With a commitment to immersion into a narrative and the richness of their experience, the following dark rides have always been a core component of Walt Disney's original formula for success.

Disneyland's Dark Rides

Peter Pan's Flight
July 17, 1955

As one of the original Disneyland dark rides, Peter Pan's Flight manifests the feeling of a childlike escape into a world of fantasy and wonderment perhaps more so than any other ride in Disneyland, and in each park where it would later appear. Though the decades since its 1955 opening have seen the development of dark rides with more impressive thrills and effects, this attraction features characters from one of Walt Disney's most beloved animated classics. With its easy-to-follow story, delightful music, and stunning imagery of worlds both real and imagined, it remains not only a signature template for the dark rides that would follow, but a popular draw for guests of all ages.

We board pirate ships running from an overhead track to set sail from the Darling family's nursery window, taking in a stunning view of moonlit Victorian London, then head off to Neverland, where we encounter the heroic Tiger Lily, the villainous Captain Hook and his bumbling henchman Mr. Smee, and the ever-present hungry crocodile. Throughout the experience, we witness many of the iconic scenes from the film, based on the J.M. Barrie novel, including the imposing Skull Rock, the Indian encampment, and Mermaid Lagoon. We then return to London and the safety of the Darling home, well out of the reach of the defeated pirates.

Like other rides in the original Fantasyland, guests were meant to take on the role of Peter Pan himself, and many did not understand this degree of immersion, expecting to see the boy who would never grow up alongside them on their adventures. Nearly three decades later, Disneyland's Fantasyland saw a major refurbishment, with many of its rides and attractions being moved or even closed. Though it would see the closing of the Pirate Ship Restaurant and the Skull Rock centerpiece outside of the attraction, elements and props from those structures, along with an audio-animatronic Peter Pan, were incorporated into the ride.

As part of the attraction's overhaul, scenes from the eventual Walt Disney World version were added, including the dueling scene aboard Hook's ship, *Jolly Roger*. This updated version of the ride would include additional animatronic figures and Peter Pan's "Come on, everybody! Here we go!"

The attraction closed again in early 2015 and would reopen later that year to celebrate the park's diamond anniversary with new animatronic figures of the Darling children and updated special effects to delight guests, from the ride queue throughout London and Neverland.

Mr Toad's Wild Ride
July 17, 1955

Based on Walt Disney's adaptation of *The Wind in the Willows*, Mr. Toad's Wild Ride is another of Disneyland's original opening-day dark rides. All the more memorable for its slightly disjointed narrative, we begin by riding an early-model motor car through the library in Toad Hall, then continue our adventure by driving through a fireplace, where glowing embers are scattered about on the floor. We then find ourselves twisting and turning into the interior of Toad Hall and through the dining room, along the way encountering Angus MacBadger, Mole, and the menacing Weasels.

The ride's interior is made of mostly two-dimensional sets, with little in the way of special effects. The increasingly destructive journey proceeds through the English countryside, drawing the attention of angry police and frightening a farmer and his livestock, and onto the docks and a warehouse full of explosives. From there, it's on to London and eventually a courthouse, where we are declared guilty by a demonic judge before being granted a reprieve and making our way to the unloading area.

While certainly not among the current crop of Disneyland's best dark rides in terms of narrative structure, scenery, or effects, Mr. Toad's Wild Ride maintains a faithful following due to its status as one of the park's few remaining inaugural attractions.

Snow White's Scary Adventures
July 17, 1955

How could Disneyland have opened without an experience based on its first and most memorable princess? Fortunately, thanks to Snow White's Scary Adventures, no one need answer that question. Like the other early dark rides within Fantasyland, Imagineers hoped to heighten guests' sense of immersion, replacing Snow White as the protagonist with the attraction's passengers as they made their way in a mining car through a re-telling the young heroine's tale, narrowly escaping the evil plans of her wicked stepmother. Disney's Imagineers were too far ahead of their time even then, as many guests did not understand why Snow White herself was featured so minimally throughout the ride.

As was the case with Peter Pan's Flight, this was remedied in Fantasyland's 1983 refurbishment, with a more deliberate insertion of Snow White within the ride. With the Wicked Queen opening her curtains every few moments to peer down at them, we enter the ride building through a façade that is meant to resemble her castle. As we make our way through the queue, a golden apple is within reach, which when touched will usher forth the queen's irksome laughter. As we progress farther into the ride, we see her spell book lying open and hinting at the dangers to come.

We board our vehicles in the quaint setting of the dwarfs' forest cottage and then come upon the dwarfs performing "The Silly Song" from the film. As we exit the cottage, we catch a brief glimpse of the queen lurking about its exterior, before making our way to the dwarfs' mine, which sparkles with the reflection of many diamonds and gems. Then we enter the queen's castle and witness her diabolical transformation into the old hag.

Skeletons warn us to turn back and flee the coming evil, as the witch prepares her poisoned apple.

We flee the castle through a frightening forest, with its natural inhabitants of trees and wildlife taking on a far more menacing visage in the dark of night. The evil cackle of the wicked hag can be heard, implying that she is close behind, as we make our way back toward the dwarfs' cottage where the hag offers us a bite of the poisoned fruit.

We then join the dwarfs in pursuit of the old hag, as she threatens to crush them (and us, watching below), with a boulder, but lightning strikes, sending her tumbling to her doom, with the screams as she falls serving as the last remnant of her wickedness.

As we exit the ride, we see that we had nothing to worry about, as Snow White is reunited with her prince and true love's kiss ensures that they live happily ever after.

Alice in Wonderland

June 14, 1958

This charmingly chaotic dark ride takes guests on a whirlwind journey through young Alice's misadventures in Wonderland, aboard caterpillar-shaped vehicles. This early addition to Disneyland's collection of dark rides was also its first to feature a brief interlude in the light of day.

A two-story dark ride, Alice in Wonderland makes use of three-dimensional sets and the film's curious characters to follow the plot of the movie, as we pursue the White Rabbit down his hole into Wonderland, where we take questionable advice from the Cheshire Cat, spin through the peculiar environment of Tulgey Wood, and witness the croquet match that sharpens the anger of the Queen of Hearts. We escape through an army of Cards to the exterior of the ride building not a moment too soon, passing by the queue of Wonderland's next visitors, before returning to the ride's final scene at the Mad Tea Party, where an enormous unbirthday cake explodes and the caterpillar ride vehicles take us to the exit.

In 1983, to enhance the theming of Fantasyland, the Mad Tea Party attraction, also inspired by *Alice in Wonderland*, was moved from its earlier location to a spot alongside the dark ride. This major renovation also saw the removal of the Upside-Down Room and the Oversized Room and the placement of the Mad Hatter's Tea Party scene at the ride's conclusion.

Until 2014, when the attraction saw an extensive retooling, it mimicked other early Disney dark rides, with the main character largely absent and guests replacing her in the narrative. Alice is now featured in a number of scenes and modern effects have been added that manage to refresh the ride without damaging its original appeal.

"it's a small world"
May 28, 1966

While other attractions might better embody the spirit of the definitive Disney dark ride with their emphasis on story, immersion into an environment, and supporting thrills and effects, there is no other that better captures the heart within the darkness. A magically merry attraction driven by a call to recognize the importance of the global community as seen through the eyes of the children of the world, "it's a small world" made its debut at the 1964-1965 New York World's Fair.

With Disney's resources already earmarked for the development of their audio-animatronic Abraham Lincoln along with other attractions for Ford and Kodak, "small world's" initial incarnation in New York was something of an afterthought of WED Enterprises that nearly did not happen. The precursor to Disney Imagineering, WED was approached by the "small world" sponsor, the Pepsi Company, with a mere six months to go before the opening of the fair. Their dedicated shop somehow made it work.

At the close of the World's Fair, the ride was dismantled and shipped across the country to Anaheim, where it would open in the spring of 1966. Voyagers on the "happiest cruise that ever sailed" board boats to visit an assortment of displays representing countries from the four corners of the earth, with dancing animatronic children singing the ride's infectious theme in their native language while dressed in traditional local costumes.

During our fifteen-minute excursion, we will see English, French, German, Belgian, Italian, Irish, and other scenes as we pass through Europe, watch mermaids and Polynesian drums as we cruise through the South Seas, hear a chorus of the infectious Sherman Brothers tune in Swedish as the boats pass through the North Pole, and visit North America and other regions, until the grand finale finds the animatronic chorus all dressed in white and singing harmoniously in English.

The voyage ends as we pass beneath a giant clock, our boats floating alongside a landscape of whimsical topiary designs of animals, until they reach the dock and we disembark.

A refurbishment that took the better part of 2008 to complete saw the addition of nearly thirty new dolls representing characters from Disney's animated legacy, from Ariel and Cinderella to Peter Pan and Pinocchio. Woody, Jessie, and Bullseye even make an appearance as the boat passes through North America.

While the attraction is certainly not dark in its tone or staging and most of the effects are comparable to those one might see in the windows of a major department store at the holidays, the narrative intent of Small World is clear and it remains at the core of Walt Disney's own words "To all who come to this happy place—welcome."

Pirates of the Caribbean
March 18, 1967

While more time will be spent discussing this and the following attraction in a subsequent chapter, it seems almost impossible to gauge the impact that Pirates of the Caribbean has had in its fifty-year history both in delighting park guests and in expanding the riches and reputation of Walt Disney Studios. Pirates was originally conceived by Walt Disney as a walk-through attraction to capitalize on the public's long standing infatuation with tales of scurvy buccaneers. After the success of "it's a small world" and its impressive capacity as a boat ride, and the equally intriguing potential for a large scale audio-animatronic attraction hinted at with the Carousel of Progress at the 1964-1965 New York World's Fair, plans for Pirates quickly shifted focus to a far more fitting water-based dark ride.

Like the Haunted Mansion and a small number of other rides, Pirates shares the rare distinction of being an attraction that inspired a film (in its case, a series of films), rather than the other way around. It is also the last attraction in which Walt Disney was involved in the design.

Featuring dazzling effects, lavish sets, and an enormous cast of audio-animatronic characters, passengers on this daring voyage witness a pirate raid, seek shelter during a ship's bombardment of a fortress, and marvel at the debauchery of its aftermath. Along the way, chance encounters with characters old and new heighten the mischief and treachery.

The Haunted Mansion
August 9, 1969

Another of the park's most iconic attractions, and one that spent more time in development than any other,the Haunted Mansion is Disneyland's answer to the creepier and more horrific haunted house dark rides offered by other amusement parks. Through the design influence of animation and Imagineering pioneer Marc Davis, a macabre sense of fun is carefully balanced with the ride's more sinister elements crafted by designer Claude Coats. Unlike modern-day fright fests and slasher flicks, every spooky thrill is delivered with a wink or clever gag, including the briefest glimpse of the attraction's narrator, whose lifeless body is seen dangling from the rafters overhead by a noose. Guests of the mansion are briefed by this now disembodied host, before boarding their Doom Buggies to meet his chilling challenge: find a way out! Long neglected by those who dwell among the living, the mansion's ghostly residents have taken full ownership, but we are told that there's room for one more.

The ride features some of Disney's most curious and ingenious special effects, as passengers carry on a search for an exit, riding through the mansion's parlor, halls, dining room, library, and attic before finding themselves in a graveyard whose residents are decidedly more spirited than most.

One of the mansion's most memorable residents is also one that has spent the least amount of time within its walls. The infamous Hatbox Ghost recently returned to dwell in his attic abode almost 45 years after a brief haunting following the attraction's 1969 opening.

Adding to the frightful fun, Disneyland's version of the Haunted Mansion is overlaid with a special holiday theme each fall. Haunted Mansion Holiday features characters, music, and elements from Tim Burton's 1991 film *The Nightmare Before Christmas*. Until the close of the winter holiday season, Jack Skellington, Sally, Oogie Boogie, and others possess every aspect of the mansion inside and out, making for an entirely different attraction.

Pinocchio's Daring Journey
May 25, 1983

A re-telling of the cherished animated classic *Pinocchio*, the dark ride experience is equal parts manic, frivolous, and heart-warming, as guests follow its titular character in his efforts to be reunited with his father, the woodcarver Geppetto.

The attraction's history at Disneyland dates back to 1976 and the removal of the Fantasyland Theater, with Pinocchio's Daring Journey planned as its replacement. However, it did not open until the major renovation of Fantasyland in 1983.

We board a woodcarver's cart and witness as Pinocchio, lured by potential fortune and glory, is unwittingly duped into serving in Stromboli's Puppet Theatre. We then see Pinocchio taken prisoner by the greedy puppeteer, but not before our cart winds up in a cage of its own. We escape, but the cart soon travels to Pleasure Island, with Pinocchio's new acquaintance, the hapless Lampwick, who is seen turning into a donkey. Other equally unwitting children are also seen depicted as donkeys, now kept within crates as punishment for their immature behavior.

Pinocchio escapes from Pleasure Island and continues his search for his father, as Monstro lunges from the depths of the sea toward the ride vehicles. Narrowly evading status as a light snack for the gigantic whale, Pinocchio is reunited with Geppetto. Under the watchful eye of the Blue Fairy, he is made a real boy as we hear the melody of "When You Wish Upon a Star."

While the ride's narrative may be somewhat difficult to follow for those unfamiliar with the film, the carnivalesque sequence on Pleasure Island is a highlight. Also, this was the first Disneyland attraction to feature holographic material, used during Lampwick's transformation, and the Pepper's Ghost illusion, most famously utilized in the Haunted Mansion's dining room scene, is used to mark the Blue Fairy's disappearance.

Splash Mountain
July 17, 1989

Though *Song of the South*, the film that inspired it, is something that the Disney company wants to banish from the collective pop culture memory, Splash Mountain is its very pleasant adaptation of the traditional mill chute dark ride based on the film's animated sequences. Audio-animatronic characters from the shuttered America Sings attraction were repurposed to populate the mountainous woodland environment. Guests follow the misadventures of Br'er Rabbit who manages to stay just one hop ahead of the meddlesome duo of Br'er Fox and Br'er Bear as he leaves home in search of his "laughing place." After multiple successful attempts to evade capture, Br'er Rabbit outwits his foes one last time by convincing them to throw him into the Briar Patch—his bayou home—as a celebratory chorus of "Zip-a-Dee-Doo-Dah" is sung by his animal friends.

Reminiscent of the many old mill and mill chute rides that inspired it, we enter the ride through an old barn. Various passages from the tales of Uncle Remus are seen on signs throughout the lengthy queue, until we board one of the six-passenger logs. We begin our journey after ascending two lifts and floating gently along a river set in Reconstruction-era Georgia.

Farm and woodland animals sing a chorus of "How Do You Do?" from a scene in the film that mixed animation with live action, and Br'er Rabbit laughs at his ability to outwit his rivals. As the musical accompaniment shifts to "Everybody Has a Laughing Place," Br'er Rabbit's confidence gets the better of him and he is trapped by Br'er Fox as our logs begin the steepest and final climb, with two predatorial vultures taunting us from above.

Before all hope is lost, Br'er Rabbit tricks his captors. As he is thrown to the safety of the briar patch, we take our own dramatic plunge, before the final chorus of "Zip-a-Dee-Doo-Dah" serves as preface to our learning that Br'er Rabbit is now safe at home, and Br'er Fox and Br'er Bear are desperately fending off a hungry alligator.

Roger Rabbit's Car Toon Spin
January 26, 1994

Situated in Mickey's Toontown, this dark ride immerses guests in the cartoon world of the 1988 film *Who Framed Roger Rabbit*.

We board a taxi cab for a tour of the city. After navigating an inventive indoor queue that takes us through Toontown's seedy back alleys and a delightful series of gags and effects, the Weasels, henchmen of Judge Doom and inspired by the menacing weasels from *The Wind in the Willows*, sabotage the path of our taxi and send it spinning uncontrollably through the Ink and Paint Club and the streets and shops of Toontown as we follow the adventures of Roger Rabbit until a climactic scene in the Gag Factory.

As much as they may be familiar with the film that inspired the attraction, guests are not so much placed in a re-telling of its story as they are immersed in the manic cartoon world of its characters. While it lacks the narrative continuity of Peter Pan's Flight or the light-hearted chills of the Haunted Mansion, this attraction's strength is in the madcap world that guests become a part of as they tag along with Roger Rabbit and his supporting cast as if they were themselves participants in an animated short.

The Indiana Jones Adventure
March 3, 1995

Ambitious by even Disney Imagineering standards, the Indiana Jones Adventure is an extraordinary example of a dark ride that invites guests into a familiar world of fantasy and fully immerses them using brilliant, state-of-the-art visual effects that support a narrative packed with nonstop action.

Initially known as Indiana Jones and the Temple of the Forbidden Eye, this dark ride was a collaboration with filmmaker George Lucas, created in response to the success of the Indiana Jones Epic Stunt Spectacular in Walt Disney World. Passengers board enhanced-motion ride vehicles that resemble jeeps to travel through a set detailed as richly as the Haunted Mansion and Pirates of the Caribbean in an attempt to locate the famed archaeologist, Dr. Jones, who has disappeared within a dangerous temple, hidden deep within the jungles of India.

The adventure begins in the queue, and if you look up as you pass through its twisting tunnels, you may encounter a hidden remnant of the old Eeyore Parking Lot that was once in its place. Winding our way through the temple's corridors, we see the hints of an archaeological expedition currently underway, until at last we enter a chamber where the setting of the experience is further explained in an old film reel, before we make our way to the loading area.

In addition to moving along its path, our ride vehicle bucks, stalls, and sways as it ventures deeper into the temple. When we encounter the Forbidden Eye, we cannot resist its gaze and are thrust into a race to locate Dr. Jones and flee the ruined temple as it collapses around us. We may encounter snakes, rats, a lava pit, and other perils that could be different each time, thanks to the ride's varying special effects that are randomly mixed through its computer control system. We encounter Indiana Jones once before the climactic scene when chased down by a massive boulder similar to the one from *Raiders of the Lost Ark*, and again as the ride nears its completion.

The Many Adventures of Winnie the Pooh
April 11, 2003

Deep in the northwest corner of the park, Many Adventures of Winnie the Pooh is a more recent dark ride in the vein of Peter Pan's Flight. Passengers are conveyed via beehives through the Hundred Acre Wood, almost as if they were turning the pages of a children's book come to life, and spend time with Eeyore, Kanga, Roo, Owl, Rabbit, Piglet, Tigger, and of course Pooh, whether contending with the toils of a blustery day, mischievous Heffalumps and Woozles, a dreadful rainstorm, or a party with Pooh, who has finally found his honey.

This attraction replaced the Country Bear Playhouse. Observant visitors can see an homage to the bears if they look up following the Heffalumps and Woozles dream sequence. The less-frequented Country Bears were a casualty to the far more popular Pooh and the park's limited room for expansion.

Buzz Lightyear's Astro Blasters
May 4, 2005

Before he knew life as a child's plaything, Buzz Lightyear enjoyed no small measure of fame as a member of Star Command, and this dark ride sees him leading guests in the charge against the evil Emperor Zurg. Buzz Lightyear's Astro Blasters is unlike any previous dark rides discussed, in that its somewhat simple plot is bolstered by the level of audience participation required, as passengers are given a degree of control of their vehicle and take up arms against Zurg and his robot minions.

As new recruits of Star Command, we board our spaceship vehicles, which are in actuality a stylized take on the omni-mover transports used in the Haunted Mansion, and add to our point tally with every successful shot at a robot until the final face-off against Emperor Zurg himself.

Monsters Inc. Mike & Sully to the Rescue!
January 23, 2006

An inspired take on revisiting the setting and characters of the Disney Pixar hit *Monsters, Inc.* that requires multiple rides to catch the many gags and visual treats crafted by the Imagineers, passengers on this dark ride join Mike and Sully as they work their way through Monstropolis in their efforts to return little Boo home safely.

After moving through a queue area themed to a bus station named the Monstropolis Transit Authority, we board taxis to begin our journey through the streets of the alternate world of Monstropolis. Taking on the roles of monsters, we learn the breaking news that a human child named Boo has been spotted within the city. As contact with humans is considered deadly, citizens of Monstropolis are naturally in a panic.

Moving onward, we pass Mike and his girlfriend, Celia, before coming upon Randall, Mike and Sully's workplace rival, angrily surveying the scene. We then see Sully holding Boo; they eventually join Mike to sneak into Monsters, Inc., but Randall has followed them. After a brief run-in with the Child Detection Agency, we proceed to the Scare Floor, where the world of the film is wonderfully brought to life, but we still have to deal with Randall. Boo hits him with a baseball bat while Mike and Sully search for her bedroom door.

After Mike and Sully say goodbye to Boo, we are decontaminated by CDA agents before encountering Mike and Sully's sluglike supervisor, Roz, who has the seeming ability to recognize guests and banter with them.

Finding Nemo Submarine Voyage
June 11, 2007

Replacing the expensive-to-operate Submarine Voyage Through Liquid Space after its nearly forty-year run, Finding Nemo Submarine Voyage takes its inspiration from the Disney-Pixar hit *Finding Nemo*.

We board a submarine in Tomorrowland to begin our descent below sea level for a lap around the lagoon beneath the Disneyland Monorail, before passing through a waterfall. The ride combines animatronics with projection effects to bring Nemo, Dory, Crush, and the story's other familiar characters to life. The visual experience of each rider differs from seat to seat, as the submarine explores shipwrecks, a school of jellyfish, and enters the mouth of a whale.

The Little Mermaid ~ Ariel's Undersea Adventure
June 3, 2011

A replica of San Francisco's Palace of Fine Arts was renovated in Disney California Adventure to resemble early 20th century aquariums when Ariel's Undersea Adventure was finally introduced as a dark ride in 2011. A dark ride based on *The Little Mermaid* had been considered for other Disney theme parks dating back to the early 1990s, and though it was scrapped, a ride-through re-creation of these initial plans was included on the platinum edition DVD release of the film.

The ride system for the realized version of the attraction is reminiscent of the Haunted Mansion, as we board clamshell cars from a continuously loading track. After a short prelude to our adventure by Ariel's confused friend Scuttle the seagull, we begin our descent under the sea, where in a series of elaborately themed aquatic scenes, Ariel's story is retold complete with versions of popular songs from the film. "Part of Your World" is enhanced by animated projections, and Sebastian the crab leads a choir of marine life through "Under the Sea" as Ariel floats in time with the rhythm.

Things begin to get more menacing when the slippery moray eels Flotsam and Jetsam offer an eerie introduction to the wicked sea witch, Ursula, who tempts Ariel with a performance of "Poor Unfortunate Souls," before casting a spell that grants her wish to be made human. Ariel's adventures on land are recounted as we hear "Kiss the Girl" as background music to her whirlwind courtship with Prince Eric. The ride ends rather abruptly as the final confrontation with Ursula seems a mere footnote before Ariel and Eric are celebrating their wedding, with King Triton's blessing.

The attraction has seen several modifications since its opening to enhance the ride experience and tweak the appearance of the characters. Ariel's hair was an early update, as guests thought it looked too phony when beneath the sea, so it now flows with a more natural sway. The projection screens that depict interstitial scenes between the audio-animatronic elements were changed from CG animation to traditional hand-drawn cels. A subsequent refurbishment saw the addition of new marine life, a view of King Triton's castle beneath the waves, additional changes to the effects, and yet more hairstyling, but this time both Ariel and Eric were given an update to make their hair appear more natural in the ride's final two scenes.

With its colorful undersea environments and catchy songs, this attraction is anything but dark, at least in tone, until Ariel's encounter with Ursula. The inventive special effects, state-of-the-art animatronics, and cleverly crafted ride vehicles make up for the somewhat rushed finale, and like Snow White's Scary Adventures, it's a reminder of the power and magic of true love, which is central to the mythology of many of Disney's animated features.

Lost in Darkness
Disneyland's Shuttered Dark Rides

Throughout its history, Disneyland has seen many rides, shows, and attractions come and go. As we learned with the construction of dark rides such as the Indiana Jones Adventure, the Many Adventures of Winnie the Pooh, Splash Mountain, and other experiences, space is at a premium in Anaheim, and more often than not, to introduce something new means bidding farewell to something old.

That is the case with the following dark rides, which were closed either due to a perceived lack of popularity or Disneyland's continued desire to innovate.

The Submarine Voyage Through Liquid Space
June 14, 1959 – September 9, 1998

Introduced at the height of the Cold War in a dull gray color and dubbed "nuclear subs," the fleet that made up the Submarine Voyage (as it was more commonly known) was inspired in part by the USS *Nautilus*, the first nuclear-powered submarine, which secretly traveled beneath the polar ice cap to become the first vessel to cross the North Pole.

The eight submarines that made up Disneyland's navy allowed as many as thirty-eight guests at a time to make their own journey to the North Pole, explore the territory of a sea serpent, the underwater world of mermaids, and the legendary lost continent of Atlantis.

The Cold War began to thaw and the submarines gained new life as their stark gray coloring was replaced with a vibrant yellow paint job. And to further enhance the experience for passengers, in the summer of 1985 female cast members dressed as mermaids and swam in the waters of the lagoon. This practice was soon discontinued, due to both the danger of the submarine motors and overeager male guests, who saw an opportunity to dive into the lagoon and try their luck with the swimming sirens.

The ride began with the submarine descending into the lagoon, where guests encountered a range of marine life, including giant clams and a shark fighting an octopus. Bubbles would simulate diving and as the submarine made its way into the show building it encountered a graveyard of lost ships and the divers attempting to plunder them for treasure, despite the threat of sharks nearby.

The journey continued to the North Pole for an encounter with a giant squid beneath the polar ice cap, before retreating to more comfortable climates where animatronic mermaids and Atlantis were explored until the threat of an underwater volcano hastened the sub onward. Soon enough, the submarine's sonar detected a strange reading: a bizarre-looking sea serpent which led the captain to believe he had spent enough time beneath the depths of the sea, whereupon he navigated the submarine back to port and the safety of Tomorrowland.

After nearly forty years, the Submarine Voyage was closed due to its low rider capacity, aged effects, and high operating costs. Its valuable park real estate would remain woefully underutilized until a young clownfish needed finding several years later.

Adventure Thru Inner Space

August 5, 1967 – September 2, 1985

Removed from Tomorrowland to make way for Star Tours, Adventure Thru Inner Space was a dark ride where guests shrunk to the size of a molecule and then to an atom, to allow them to imagine the world from the perspective of a tiny fragment of a snowflake. Imperiled by tiny errant electrons and other dangers afforded by their simulated new stature, they explored the elements of nature until the prospect of shrinking small enough to travel within the nucleus of an atom proved too great a risk and they returned to their original size.

Owing its origins to designs dating back to the mid-1950s and plans for a Tomorrowland expansion to be dubbed Science Land, which might have included additional attractions about time travel, space exploration, and other themes at the forefront of scientific theory in the era, the ride saw its plans put on hold due to the time required by the Imagineers to focus on the 1964-1965 New York World's Fair.

When realized in its 1967 version, Adventure Thru Inner Space was sponsored by Monsanto, a partnership that lasted for its first decade. Its centerpiece was the Monsanto Mighty Microscope, which provided the means of shrinkage. Especially innovative for being the first ride to use Disney's new omnimover system, dubbed "atommobiles" in this incarnation, the vehicles conveyed passengers through the microscope so they could then watch as the surrounding snowflakes grew larger and larger, then smaller and smaller. The Sherman Brothers, the sibling composers behind countless classic Disney songs, and countless others, penned "Miracles from Molecules" to open and close the ride experience.

Even today, sharp-eyed guests can catch a glimpse of the Mighty Microscope as it lives on in Star Tours: The Adventures Continue.

Superstar Limo
February 8. 2001 – January 11, 2002

This short-lived dark ride was part of the opening day offerings at Disney California Adventure, but closed not quite a year later to be replaced by Monsters, Inc. Mike & Sully to the Rescue!

Arriving at Los Angeles International Airport, guests assumed the role of the Hollywood elite on their way to the star-studded premiere of their latest film. After boarding a limo, they were escorted to several California hotspots, including Beverly Hills, the Sunset Strip, Bel Air, and Malibu, and between collect calls from a slimy Hollywood agent, enjoyed B-list celebrity sightings ranging from Regis Philbin, Antonio Banderas, and Melanie Griffith, to Tim Allen, Jackie Chan, and Drew Carey. Adding to the fun, Madame Leota made a brief appearance, attempting to summon good news from a studio executive. Finally, after a rush of paparazzi notice their arrival, Whoopi Goldberg greeted guests at Mann's Chinese Theatre. As they pass by the souvenir photos made available from their ride, they receive a final call from their agent, predicting stardom.

Navigating the Darkness
Ride Vehicles, Capacity and Queueing

Perhaps the design element that has left the most iconic and lasting mark on Disney theme parks since first introduced so ingeniously at Disneyland is the hub-and-spoke model of spatial navigation. This method of crowd control, which to varying degrees serves as the standard for many Disney parks around the world with minimal modification, is designed to resemble a wheel, with a hub, such as Sleeping Beauty Castle at its center, and multiple spokes, or pathways, leading to the surrounding lands and entirely different adventures, designed to minimize congestion by controlling crowds with a minimum of intersecting walkways.

Disney Imagineers understand that before even boarding a ride vehicle, guests' senses are already building a story, using the landscape, sounds, and even scents they encounter to enhance their experience; therefore, they have gone to considerable effort to extend these sensory experiences as much as possible and often in a very deliberate order and pacing.

Using design techniques such as forced perspective to manipulate park goers, instilling them with a sense of awe at the park's size as they arrive, and comfort at its relative smallness as they leave, Disney's engineers have employed similar artistry when crafting the façades of their dark rides. Like its many other elements, the architecture of the Disney theme park is meant to transport guests to another time or place away from the mundane nature of reality. Turrets are common. Windows are larger and mouldings are ornately designed. Certain design elements might be exaggerated to make guests feel more like they are actually there. Though it would not open until years after it was built, the exterior of

the Haunted Mansion stood complete with playfully macabre
signs posted at its gate hinting to what was coming. Visitors
are meant to believe that the Wicked Queen truly may be
lurking within her castle and that Jack Sparrow may at any
moment come running through Adventureland, so these environments must be made to accommodate those possibilities.

These gateways to adventure must not only invite guests
into whatever world Imagineers have built within, they must
be functional as part of the narrative. Strip away the artistry
covering any typical façade and you are essentially left with
a soundstage inside the show building. It is equally important that this reality should be made as invisible as possible
to guests.

Of course one element that is often beyond the control of
even Disney's talented engineers is that of its often endless
ride queues. While park guests can be directed toward a central
monument and will naturally gravitate toward those attractions
they most enjoy, it is challenging to control the high volume of
visitors, especially in areas where space is at a premium.

As lines are one of the most undesirable aspects of the
guest experience, Disney attraction designers have employed
a number of strategies to alleviate some of this frustration.
One way they have done this is by concealing the lines within
the show buildings. As a line forms, it is kept out of sight and
out of the way of those passing by the attraction, while those
inside zig zag and back and forth through seemingly endless
passages. As guests amble toward the loading area, it can
almost become a social experience as they encounter the same
faces again and again at every turn, waiting in shared anticipation. Some attractions even feature optional post-shows that
continue the shared experience after disembarking, sometimes offering an educational element, a plug from a corporate
sponsor, or simply a way for guests to gradually acclimate to
the larger world outside of the attraction.

Imagineers would certainly not leave guests to their own
devices with wait times for some of the more popular attractions exceeding three hours, and in recent years have enhanced
waiting areas with a variety of new and interactive elements.
Generally speaking, queue and loading areas have always been

themed to fit an attraction's narrative, using architectural elements, murals, and other principles of design to engage guests and enhance the storytelling, and much like their animated cinematic counterparts, would draw viewers in as their anticipation builds, though in this case instead of watching the drama unfold on-screen, they become active participants.

So it is before guests have even entered a queue that engagement begins. Understanding full well that the best of Disney's dark rides take guests on an emotional journey as much as a physical one, and that it is imperative to keep them from experiencing any sense boredom even while doing something as mundane as waiting in line, what is ordinarily a tedious and forgettable process is now something memorable.

Approaching a fairly recent attraction like Under the Sea ~ Journey of the Little Mermaid in Magic Kingdom's Fantasyland, the feeling that you do not simply ride a Disney attraction but *participate* in it is evident. Nearing the entrance to Prince Eric's castle through an underground cavern, you pass a waterfall and hear music that you think would not be out of place on any ship at sea. Rather than hide the impending toil of a hum-drum line, the queue has been constructed so that guests walk through artfully designed caverns and can participate in a scavenger hunt with Ariel's crustacean guardian, Sebastian, before being welcomed by cast members dressed in nautically themed attire to board their clamshell vehicles.

Similar enhancements have also enlivened the wait times for many of Disney's classic dark rides following periods of refurbishment, including the interactive queue at Orlando's Haunted Mansion and additions to Peter Pan's Flight that have set Tinker Bell and Peter Pan's shadow loose in the Darling family's nursery and allow guests to cast their own shadow throughout the room while "wearing" character costumes and interacting with objects or each other.

In his book *Designing Disney*, Imagineer John Hench cites the Indiana Jones Adventure as one of the best queues ever designed:

> It offers both story elements of the single-line pre-show together with an occasional, sociability-inducing switch-back. It introduces story elements with a clear sense of

progression, reinforcing the ride itself. The queue makes guests feel that they are already part of the experience as they approach the boarding area.

We will see as our discussion of individual attractions continues that the queuing process may also include audio-animatronic elements, video pre-shows, and other efforts that serve not only to orient guests to whatever ride it is that they are about to experience, but also to maintain their enthusiasm.

Once guests have made it through the queue, they next encounter the loading area, where they board a stylized ride vehicle to begin their adventure. Attraction designers have long endeavored to make these vehicles fit within the narrative they have created, especially for the earliest dark rides where guests were meant to take on the role of characters from the films that inspired the rides, whether careening through Toad Hall in a motorcar or taking flight over London in a pirate galleon.

Indeed, these dark ride attractions are meant to immerse you in the world of your favorite Disney film, whisk you to far-off lands or undersea kingdoms, or transport you to another place in time. Like the sights and sounds of an attraction's façade and enriched queue experiences, to varying degrees ride vehicles can play a part in enhancing the story experience the Imagineers are trying to tell, both aesthetically and functionally.

Imagineers must first decide the type of attraction they want to deliver and that will influence its design. Take, for example, the origins of Splash Mountain. Owing its roots to one of the earliest amusement park attractions, Splash Mountain's vehicles, themed to resemble logs, are a descendant of the old mill and log flume rides dating back to the late 19th century. In the 1980s, corporate interests called for the introduction of a log flume ride in Disneyland. The potential for recycling many of the similarly styled audio-animatronics from the unpopular America Sings attraction led Imagineer Tony Baxter to consider using the animated characters from Disney's 1946 film *Song of the South* as inspiration for the attraction, rather than the attraction's story driving the design.

In part for simplicity's sake, some of Disney's best examples of this story-driven design may be their earliest and simplest dark rides, where guests are inserted into the environment of a familiar animated tale and either witness elements of a familiar story unfold or take on, in a way, the role of its lead characters. In Peter Pan's Flight, much like the Darling children, we take flight from the nursery window, soaring over the London sky before arriving in Neverland to meet its mysterious and exotic inhabitants and do battle with pirates. It is only fitting that we, like Wendy, John, and Michael, spend at least part of our journey aboard a flying pirate galleon. In a world that is not limited by the confines of today, but open to yesterday, tomorrow, and fantasy, the manner in which we explore these realms is nearly as expansive as the places Imagineers can take us.

There are, however, a number of ride systems that designers will call on to best serve their storytelling needs. The earliest of these, and most common among Disney's classic attractions, are track systems, which facilitate the storytelling process by creating a predetermined route through an enclosed space. Moving along an electrified rail, this type of vehicle allowed ride operators to control its speed and to start and stop it during specific sections of an attraction, making it an ideal option for guests to experience narrative dark rides. Examples of this type of attraction include Snow White's Scary Adventures, Mr. Toad's Wild Ride, Roger Rabbit's Car Toon Spin, Monsters, Inc. Mike & Sully to the Rescue!, and The Many Adventures of Winnie the Pooh.

For less earthbound attractions, track ride systems may also be suspended from the ceiling. Peter Pan's Flight is an early example of this variation and Tokyo DisneySea's 20,000 Leagues Under the Sea employs the same approach to simulate a deep sea dive, with its ride vehicles designed to look like submersible craft.

Water rides, such as "it's a small world," Pirates of the Caribbean, and Epcot's Frozen Ever After, which are typically powered by pumps or currents, may also make use of tracks to some extent, as well as lifts and inclines to build momentum.

When Imagineers do choose to take us beneath the ocean, the ride vehicle is partially submerged and uses a variety of effects to simulate aquatic life. Disney's many flirtations with the stories of Jules Verne and more recently the animated film *Finding Nemo* are examples of this type of attraction.

Disneyland's success was immediate. As attendance continued to grow throughout the late 1950s and early 1960s, so too did Walt's interest in attractions that could handle the ever-increasing crowds. A people eating answer came in the form of the omnimover. According to David Younger, in *Theme Park Design*:

> The omnimover was developed to achieve two main goals: to utilize a looped chain of vehicles that never stop so as to dramatically increase the ride capacity, and to have a rotatable ride vehicle that allows precise control over the ride vehicle's sightlines.

The dome-shaped vehicles control their passengers' line of sight, allowing designers greater control over the sequencing of story elements and the inclusion of onboard speakers may offer an even more individualized rider experience. The Haunted Mansion is no doubt the most iconic example of this type of vehicle, but it was not the first: Adventure Thru Inner Space predated its opening by over two years. Phantom Manor in Disneyland Paris, The Little Mermaid ~ Ariel's Undersea Adventure, Horizons, and If You Had Wings are just a few additional dark ride attractions to take advantage of the innovations offered by this high-volume ride system.

Imagineers would continue to innovate after the omnimover with the introduction of a modified version that allows for interactivity on a number of dark rides, including the Buzz Lightyear series of shooting games.

In some cases, even the innovations offered by the omnimover have proven insufficient for the level of immersion hoped for by the Imagineers and so additional options have been created to meet this need. Monsters. Inc. Ride & Go Seek! in Tokyo Disneyland uses a 360-degree turning vehicle to allow for interactive dark ride gameplay, having adapted its ride system from Toy Story Midway Mania.

Still another ride type is the enhanced motion vehicle, or EMV. Attractions such as DINOSAUR, Indiana Jones Adventure, and Indiana Jones and the Temple of the Crystal

Skull feature stylized vehicles mounted on motion platforms which function much like a simulator ride, albeit mobile. Motion effects are transmitted to the EMV offering a number of variant ride possibilities each time.

One of Disney's most recent innovations in dark ride navigation is the trackless ride system, utilized in attractions such as Pooh's Hunny Hunt, Mystic Manor, and Ratatouille: The Adventure. Using GPS, RFID, or other navigation technologies rather than a set rail to guide vehicles through the ride space, trackless attractions offer the potential of new and unique ride paths and changes in speed and timing all managed by a guidance system, in service to enhancing the story.

In keeping with the desire to build on what they have done before, Disney's newest version of their long-time classic dark ride, Pirates of the Caribbean, dubbed Pirates of the Caribbean: Battle of the Sunken Treasure, uses an innovative new ride system allowing them to start, stop, and change the direction of boats at will, which had not been possible in earlier versions of the iconic boat ride.

As prolific as the creative talent of the Disney company has been throughout the course of their nearly seven decades in the theme park industry, the successes they have achieved are not entirely their own. Arguably one of Walt's most important partners in realizing his dream of Disneyland was Arrow Development, who as one of Disney's earliest collaborators had a direct impact on a number of the company's most memorable dark rides along with many other attractions.

During World War II, the Santa Clara Valley, in a region of California that was predominantly farmland, began to take on increasing significance in the aerospace and electronics industries, according to the 2016 documentary *The Legacy of Arrow Development*. After the war, four men decided to go into business for themselves in Mountain View, California. Ed Morgan, Karl Bacon, Angus Anderson, and William Hardiman spent the late 1940s selling machine tools, doing automotive repair and restoration, and building models.

Their design work on a children's amusement park in San Jose drew the attention of others in this industry, and as word of the quality of their work spread, it eventually reached Walt Disney, who would award them a contract to assist in the design of Mr. Toad's Wild Ride, Snow White's Scary Adventures, and other opening day attractions, for $250,000. Disney considered the dark rides he experienced at other amusement parks too noisy for what he was trying to accomplish in his park. "We're trying to tell a story in those rides; we need quiet cars," he once observed.

In the years to come, Disney would partner with Arrow on several attractions, including the Alice in Wonderland dark ride and the Matterhorn Bobsleds. Disney's team of Imagineers would control the design process and Arrow took care of the manufacture and installation of ride systems that were not only more silent than their competition, but also featured the degree of maneuverability required by the Imagineers. Melody Malmberg, in *Walt Disney Imagineering*, wrote:

> After construction of the Matterhorn, Disney bought a third of Arrow Development, and moved the company to a larger plant at 1555 Plymouth Street in the North Bayshore Area. At the new location Arrow went on to develop new ride systems for Disney, and developed the vehicles and tracks for "it's a small world," Pirates of the Caribbean, Adventure Through Inner Space, and the Haunted Mansion.

Arrow would build or enhance a number of attractions for Disney as well as develop their own projects and rides for other amusement parks, including England's Blackpool Pleasure Beach, which decades earlier had seen the debut of Emberton's Ghost Train. They had a period of tremendous success due in no small part to their association with Disney and would go on to design attractions for Knott's Berry Farm, King's Island, Cedar Point, Six Flags, Dollywood, and countless other parks, before filing for bankruptcy in 2001 and shutting down the following year.

Disney would then partner with a number of other companies, outsourcing the engineering component of its dark rides to varying degrees, but none would match the immediate and lasting impact on the company's legacy of Arrow Development.

The most memorable Disney dark rides are carefully staged to show guests only what the designers want them to see. In his article "Arrow Development," Nick Perry wrote: "Imagineers search for a story, or a part of a story, that can be told experientially and in three dimensions." Using immersive world building, creative queueing, and the method of conveyance that best serves the story, the intent is to offer guests a sensory experience that mirrors that of the characters brought to life by the attraction. Like Ariel, we journey fathoms below the ocean's depths to delight in her adventures in Under the Sea ~ Journey of the Little Mermaid, and in Peter Pan's Flight, we are all but dared to join Peter Pan and take off to Neverland to experience with the Darling children the sensation of flying through the nighttime sky of London and beyond.

CHAPTER FOUR

World's Fairs, Pirates, and Happy Haunts

Long considered opportunities for nations to showcase achievement and celebrate the intermingling of cultures and ideas, world's fairs had presented innovations in science, technology, and spectacle for generations before Walt Disney's birth. Though they would be billed by varying designations and could be of vastly different scope, such as the 1901 Pan American Exposition in Buffalo, New York, which played host to Frederic Thompson's ground-breaking dark ride A Trip To The Moon, or the 1893 World's Columbian Exhibition in Chicago, which commemorated the 400th anniversary of Christopher Columbus' arrival in the New World and counted Elias Disney, Walt's father, among the many laborers involved in its construction, fairs commonly brought people together for education and amusement.

Elias shared his stories of working on the fair with young Walt, from the breadth and diversity of the international pavilions and spectacle of the exhibitions highlighting new technology, to how the fair was mapped out. These stories would remain with Walt for the rest of his life.

Numerous biographers, along with Walt himself, have suggested that Elias Disney was a hard man, who instilled within his son not only his ambitious vision, but the drive and work ethic to realize it. Ambition is so often paired with opportunity, and Walt understood that the next world's fair would be a chance not only to test the potential appeal of a Disneyland style park on the east coast, but to do so with new and innovative attractions created on someone else's dime. This would not be the first time in Walt's life that a world's fair would come calling. Walt's biographer Neil Gabler, in *Walt Disney: The Triumph of the American Imagination*, wrote:

> Walt had produced a four-minute Mickey Mouse cartoon for the Nabisco pavilions at the San Francisco and New York World's Fairs in 1939 and the coordinator of the United States pavilion at the 1958 World's Fair in Brussels had asked Walt to design an attraction there.

This would result in the popular Circarama film *America the Beautiful*, reused to similar success the following year in Moscow. Turning down an initial proposal to develop attractions for a Children's Village by city planner Robert Moses, which he feared would prove unprofitable, Walt instead recruited Disney artist Herb Ryman to assist with the realization of his vision for Disney's contribution to the fair, believing that forward-thinking companies would want an exhibition that drew attention to their products in a way that set them apart from others and used state-of-the-art technology to create a buzz. In *Walt Disney's Imagineering Legends and the Genesis of the Disney Theme Park*, Jeff Kurtti wrote:

> Presenting ideas to corporations and government entities—not exactly renowned as hotbeds of creative discourse—required exactly the kind of visual story impression Ryman could create in a single image.

Armed with his stable of talented Imagineers and the proof of concept that was Disneyland, Walt began approaching corporate leaders about potential partnerships as early as 1960. Their efforts secured relationships with Ford Motor Company, General Electric, Pepsi-Cola, and the State of Illinois.

With the theme of "Progress Through Understanding," the fair was set to open in Flushing Meadows, Queens, on April 22, 1964. While developing new attractions for the fair would prove a unique opportunity, it had the downside of sidelining many projects currently planned for Walt's own park. As he had for Disneyland before it, Walt would draw from the ranks of his talented team of animators turned Imagineers to translate his storytelling methods to this new experiment. Ryman, Harriet Burns, Claude Coats, Marc Davis, Rolly Crump, Sam McKim, and many others would all lend their skills to the creativity, research, and development poured into what would rank among the most popular attractions at the fair.

Commissioned by the State of Illinois, the Imagineers used animation provided by Marc Davis to bring to life an audio-animatronic representation of America's sixteenth president for Great Moments with Mr. Lincoln. According to Alyssa Carnahan, writing for waltdisney.org:

> The figure was capable of more than 250,000 combinations of movement, including motion of the arms, legs, and mouth. The animatronic Lincoln performed for audiences five times per hour, and looked so lifelike that some audiences thought he was played by a live actor.

Marc Davis' knowledge of anatomy was essential in creating a convincing illusion of realistic human movement. The alarmingly lifelike representation of Lincoln was also largely due to the sculpture work of Imagineer and sculptor Blaine Gibson, who had spent years honing his craft, and after this spectacularly convincing effort, would go on to create characters for Pirates of the Caribbean, Haunted Mansion, Hall of Presidents, Country Bear Jamboree, and other memorable attractions.

Though audio-animatronic technology had already been used in Disneyland's Enchanted Tiki Room, the advances made while perfecting the full-size Abraham Lincoln figure would prove invaluable when work resumed on Pirates of the Caribbean. Progressive as he was even in this form, audio-animatronic Lincoln was not without its problems, as Jeff Kurtti wrote:

> Since the Lincoln figure was not ready to perform prior to his debut (nor did Walt want to lose the "premiere" impact of the unique audio-animatronics presentation), Walt and [show-writer] James Algar presented the Lincoln show to fair officials and dignitaries from the State of Illinois just as they would "walk through" the story of an animated feature—as a series of storyboards, with McKim's drawings of Lincoln "performing" his speech in lieu of the mechanical figure.

McKim's detailed paintings would also provide an engrossing guide for guests in the attraction's pre-show.

Marc Davis' design work would also play a part in General Electric's Carousel of Progress, where his humorous approach matched the attraction's mix of nostalgia and futurism as guests explore technological advances as seen through the eyes of generations of a family from the early 1900s through the dawn of the 21st century. Its story was encapsulated in the song "There's a Great Big Beautiful Tomorrow," penned by brothers Richard M. and Robert B. Sherman, which was as much Walt Disney's manifesto on the future as it was a way to hold the shifting eras of the show together thematically through music.

Davis would also contribute art that inspired the charming and humorous sequences in Ford's Magic Skyway, a journey through humanity's history from the days of dinosaurs through the Space Age, and would collaborate with studio artist turned children's book illustrator Mary Blair on "it's a small world," an attraction designed for the fair's UNICEF pavilion, sponsored by Pepsi-Cola. With less than nine months to go before the start of the fair, Walt asked Blair back to revisit the stylized drawings of Mexican children that she had created for a sequence in the animated film *The Three Caballeros*. Davis' characters and settings blended seamlessly with her whimsical concept art and with Rolly Crump's oversized props that filled the scenes. Davis' wife, Alice, would create the many costumes needed for the dolls featured throughout the attraction, and with the help of Herb Ryman, Rolly Crump, Blaine Gibson, and other Imagineers, their fanciful designs were soon brought to life in three dimensions. The Sherman Brothers were called on once again to compose music for the boat ride, and the attraction's eponymous theme song has since been called the most translated and performed song on earth.

Not only would this attraction prove an instant classic in its own right, the boats and propulsion method used to convey ten million guests throughout the fair's two-year run would inspire designers to scrap plans for the still-in-development Pirates of the Caribbean walk-through attraction and similarly reimagine it as a boat ride. Jeff Kurtti wrote that Imagineer Claude Coats, who like many of his peers divided time developing multiple attractions for the fair, "remembered coming back from the fair and hearing that the 'pirate museum' walk-through was now going to be a water flume ride like 'it's a small world.' Coats' experience fitting ten pounds of attraction into a five-pound bag in the Fantasyland dark rides was immediately put to use."

With the precedent established years before in the months leading up to Disneyland's opening, Walt previewed the World's Fair attractions on "Disneyland Goes to the World's Fair," which aired on May 17, 1964, as part of his weekly NBC series, *Walt Disney's Wonderful World of Color*. Just as television audiences had been enticed to the Magic Kingdom by early hints of Frontierland, Fantasyland, and other weekly glimpses of what was to come in the mid-1950s, Walt used this opportunity to showcase the massive audio-animatronic Tyrannosaurus Rex, Triceratops, and other dinosaurs that featured prominently in Ford's Magic Skyway, and an assortment of the seven hundred dolls that would appear in "it's a small world." Remarking on the admiration for Abraham Lincoln he had felt since his boyhood in Illinois, Walt would note how he "wanted to bring to the people of today the inspiring words of the man who held this nation together during its moment of greatest crisis—the Civil War" before moving on to showcase a model of the Carousel of Progress. Typical of Disney's television programs, this special highlighted not only the attractions themselves, but the technology behind them and the sponsors who made them possible, while also spending a few fleeting moments with the Imagineers and others responsible for their creation.

In his memoir, Rolly Crump recalled:

> None of us knew we were going to bring this back to Disneyland. We didn't realize the true significance of all these shows until Walt called us in one day and said, "We own them, so we're going to bring them back and we're going to put them in Disneyland."

At the conclusion of the fair, Disney's four attractions were packed and shipped west for installation at Disneyland. Great Moments with Mr. Lincoln was the first to debut, taking up residence in the Disneyland Opera House on Main Street in July 1965. An updated version of "it's a small world," with a new façade, clock face, and modified interior, opened in Fantasyland in May 1966. Two months later, audio-animatronic dinosaurs from Ford's Magic Skyway became part of the Primeval World diorama seen by passengers aboard the Disneyland Railroad. Finally, in July 1967, the Carousel of Progress opened as part of the updated Tomorrowland, where it would remain until opening in Walt Disney World in 1975.

John Hench, who contributed to the development of all of the Disney attractions at the fair, noted that their success would not have been remotely possible without Walt's guidance:

> So decisions were being made all the time because Walt was there and he made those fast decisions. Even with Lincoln... I thought he'd never work. To me it was just like Walt had willed him to. Walt had to apologize to the press two or three times saying, 'We're just not ready yet'—and one day, we were ready.

But the risks that Walt took in lending his name and the resources of his studio would pay off well beyond these four hit attractions and even beyond the breakthroughs made for the still-gestating Pirates of the Caribbean and Haunted Mansion dark rides. Encouraged by the unqualified success of their time at the World's Fair, which like Disneyland itself was yet another example of a massive influx of people access-ing limited attractions in a limited space, Disney executives took careful note of anything that could inform their own best practices when it came to the flow of guests through the various pavilions, capacity, queueing, storytelling, show design, transportation technology, and how to design ride experiences to quickly ingest as many guests as possible.

The Tales That Dead Men Tell

Over the course of a weekend of frantic activity in late 1953, with Walt looking over his shoulder, Herb Ryman would sketch out in pencil Walt's vision of his most comprehensive conceptualization to date of what would become Disneyland. Only days later, Roy Disney would use these sketches to help convince skeptical financial backers of the potential in his brother's latest dream.

This early design included everything from a storybook castle, a pirate galleon, and a working farm to a city of tomorrow, a Mississippi paddle boat, and an exotic African village.

Yet even as the park gates opened to the public less than two years later, Walt would continue enhancing his visionary theme park, constantly looking for new ways to enrich the guest experience, and as interest in the park grew and attendance along with it, address the issue of his need to accommodate the increased capacity.

Defying the expectations of Walt's early skeptics, Disneyland would see its first major expansion in 1959, with the opening of the Matterhorn Bobsleds, the Submarine Voyage, and the monorail. Yet as much as he would look ahead with these exciting new additions in and around Tomorrowland, Walt remained equally enchanted with the romance and adventure of America's frontier past.

Beginning in the late 1950s as a way to better utilize a patch of land at the bend of the Rivers of America, Disneyland's New Orleans Square went through numerous conceptual changes as it evolved from the planning stages to its final design. As the last major project overseen by Walt Disney and the first new section of the park to open since the original five lands, it would eventually play host to two of Disney's most endearing dark rides: Pirates of the Caribbean and The Haunted Mansion.

Bringing the Crescent City to life within the confines of the Magic Kingdom was a lengthy process of planning, design, and realization, lasting from the initial discussions in 1957 and groundbreaking four years later, to its grand opening in the summer of 1966. This protracted period of development allowed for innovation within Disney's Imagineering department to flourish. With nearly a decade passing between concept to result, it gave many different artists an opportunity to contribute to the style, atmosphere, and design of this waypoint between Adventureland and Frontierland.

In *Pirates of the Caribbean: From the Magic Kingdom to the Movies*, Jason Surrell writes:

> In an ominous hint of adventures to come, a beached pirate ship, with treasure chests overflowing with gold and jewels and loot scattered around the remnants of a sea battle, lent a distinct pirate overlay to the area. In fact, one of the first renderings of just such a New Orleans-themed area (then envisioned as a subset of Adventureland, or "True-Life Land)" as it is labeled on the drawing) pre-dates the opening of the park with Herb Ryman's 1954 concept sketch depicting a "Pirate Shack" and "Bluebeard's Den."

What was initially meant to attract investors would by 1958 be considered far enough along in the planning stages to appear on Disneyland souvenir maps as New Orleans Square, with promises of a Wax Museum and Thieves Market, among other intriguing diversions. Largely on the strength of Herb Ryman's designs, progress would continue on the development of New Orleans Square, with Imagineers set to work on bringing to life Walt's romanticized aesthetics of the region and period—understanding, as ever, that its look would contribute to the mood and experience of guests as they explored the avenues of this curious new neighborhood.

A short time later, Marc Davis had recently completed his latest masterwork, the vile Cruella De Vil, from *101 Dalmations*, and found himself looking for a new project. One of Disney's revered "Nine Old Men," Davis had been with the Disney studio since 1935 and had since become one of its most respected character designers. Recognizing his talent, Walt asked Davis to travel to Anaheim to take a look at an attraction up for potential refurbishment. Impressed by his take on the ride, Disney would task him with a number of additional Imagineering roles, including a revamp of the Jungle Cruise, where Davis' knack for gags would quickly become apparent, and he found himself involved with other projects.

In 1961, after more than half a decade of stumbles, sputters, and debates on the direction of its design, construction finally began on Disneyland's take on the Delta City. Walt assigned Davis to work on a pirate wax museum. Conceived as a walk-through attraction, it was entirely different from that of the familiar fairy-tale characters nearby in Fantasyland. It would be a world of untoward avarice and cunning, of crafty buccaneers and shadowy scoundrels. Here, guests would step further into the dark side of Disneyland. But how dark was too dark for Disney?

Doing background research for the wax museum, Davis would soon discover that the real-life stories of these buccaneers were not the type of thing that the family-friendly Disney organization wished to share with its guests. Surrell wrote:

> They would have to sign the pirate's contractual articles with their own blood. It turns out that there were very few battles with pirates at sea. Most pirates died of venereal disease that they got in bawdy houses in various coastal towns.

Given the disturbing nature of their backstories and Davis' own predilection for humor, he decided to stray from the more unsavory aspects of reality and infuse the experience with humor wherever possible.

Still, as with any Disney attraction, the intent was to up the ante considerably. Walking through this wax museum, guests would find themselves immersed in the world of pirates, with intricate tableaux revealing secluded grottos, an island treasure hunt, a moored pirate ship, and of course the pirates themselves, posed to populate these elaborate scenes. According to Surrell:

> In one of the earliest walk-through versions of the show, a guide would lead fifty to seventy guests at a time through six or so different vignettes, telling the story depicted in each scene. The Disneyland operations team quickly concluded that it would be difficult to retain the attention of such a large group and decided to let guests gather on their own and then begin the spiel.

This approach led to Disney's ever-present concern for capacity, which would be abated as interest shifted toward making Pirates a more efficiently paced attraction, where guests would instead be conveyed through scenes in some way.

As much as the progress made by the Imagineers during the period leading up to the 1964-1965 New York World's Fair would eventually inform Pirates of the Caribbean, while their focus shifted eastward to the fair, work on Disneyland attractions effectively stopped.

Spurred by the success of their four hit attractions from the World's Fair, Walt and his Imagineers returned to Anaheim eager to implement what they had learned back east. In addition to Great Moments with Mr. Lincoln, the Imagineers would introduce the Carousel of Progress, the Magic Skyway, and "it's a small world." Despite the delay in forward momentum as New York took precedence, the advances in technology developed for these new attractions contributed immediately to progress on Pirates of the Caribbean and would continue to bear fruit for Disney's theme park attractions for decades to come.

The ability of Disney's Imagineers to produce such a convincingly human audio-animatronic re-creation of Abraham Lincoln facilitated their work on an entire cast of audio-animatronic pirate characters that would sack their way through a 17th-century seaport town.

Having learned many lessons during their time in New York, the Imagineers also took to heart the need to meet the increase in guest demand that would result from the addition of any new and hopefully popular rides. Arrow Development, which had played such a key role in Disneyland's early years, contributing as they did to Snow White's Scary Adventures and Mr. Toad's Wild Ride, among other attractions, created the ride system for "it's a small world"—which, with proper theming, would seem a perfect fit for a ride-through adventure featuring seafaring scalawags. Not only would a water-based ride serve the attraction's narrative, but with its ability to accommodate thousands of guests per hour, it would keep unsightly lines at a minimum.

In contrast to the dark rides of Fantasyland, which inserted guests into already familiar cinematic worlds and then whisked them through retellings of stories they had known for years, this new attraction, Pirates, without a film or fairy tale as its source material, lacked a specific frame of reference. Therefore, the sense of immersion felt by guests would matter considerably more, as without the familiar narrative of an animated feature such as *Pinocchio* to serve as the basis for the attraction, the concept began as a series of interconnected vignettes to give passengers the *idea* of pirates as they floated through the darkened grottos and burning town, with clever gags and effects to further enliven each scene.

While Marc Davis labored over the attraction's humorous elements, background painter Claude Coats, who had worked on a number of classic animated features before joining the Imagineering team in 1955, focused his efforts on the interior design of the ride, including its Caribbean setting. He would be joined by fellow Imagineer Yale Gracey, whose mechanical wizardry would lend itself to many of the attraction's special effects, most notably the foreboding night sky that would greet passengers as they sailed off into the lagoon and the climactic scene of the burning seaport. Gracey's fire effect would turn out to be so convincing that Anaheim's fire chief requested that it be programmed to shut down in the event of an actual fire.

As the attraction's characters and setting gradually solidified, Walt turned to Xavier "X" Atencio to craft its story. Having joined the Disney studio in 1938 to assist with the production of *Fantasia*, Atencio was hand-picked by Walt for Imagineering, and with little practical experience as a storyman, tasked with scripting this ambitious new attraction. To prepare himself, he referred back not only to Disney's 1950 live-action *Treasure Island*, but a variety of classic pirate films, including *Captain Blood*, *Blackbeard the Pirate*, and *The Sea Hawk*. This cinematic inspiration was intentional. "We do try to use the material that's in film, because people know it and recognize it," noted John Hench in a 1984 episode of *Disney Family Album*. Like the Fantasyland dark rides, giving guests a connection with something familiar enhanced the level of engagement Imagineers were seeking, as these recognizable story elements, whether a wooden leg, eye patch, or a heavily accented pattern of speech, allowed them to bring guests into the narrative.

Atencio would face concerns similar to those of Davis. When scripting the attraction's scenes, he encountered scenarios not appropriate for Disneyland. From sacking and looting to murder and auctioning off voluptuous red-headed women, the vignettes had to be introduced in such a way that guests of all ages would recognize that the pirates were really just light-hearted, fun-loving rascals

As guests board their pirate galleons and take flight over London en route to Neverland on Peter Pan's Flight, they do so to the familiar melody of "You Can Fly." And even as they watch Pinocchio succumbing to the temptations of Pleasure Island while bearing witness to Pinocchio's Daring Journey, the pleasant tune "Hi-Diddle-Dee-Dee (An Actor's Life for Me)" is heard. Like the characters and films that inspired them, these songs had already become classics by the time they were made part of the soundtrack of their dark ride counterparts, so it was only natural that Pirates of the Caribbean be given the same treatment, as the music would serve to not only create a sense of continuity throughout the vignettes, along with the gags and the dialogue created for the scenes, but soften some of the more unsettling imagery. Novice songwriter Atencio wrote the lyrics to "Yo Ho (A Pirate's Life For Me)," with music by George Bruns, who had written "The Ballad of Davy Crockett" years earlier.

With its story, scenes, and setting in place, it would soon be time for the pirates themselves to be brought to life. Marc Davis' characters were first taken from the page and into three-dimensional life by sculptor Blaine Gibson. Gibson's craft was a careful mix of reality and embellishment. The studio would often use composite elements of real people in their character designs to heighten believability. Gibson explained:

> In a ride system, you only have a few seconds to say something about a figure through your art. So we exaggerate their features, especially their facial features, so they can be quickly and easily understood from a distance. If you examined them closely, you'd find the nose, the cheekbones, the eyes all somewhat exaggerated. The frowns and the grins are all exaggerated, too, because we have to instantly communicate "good guy" or "bad guy." We try to provide the illusion of life.

Layer by layer, the models were built over wire skeletons until they matched Davis' drawings. Gibson and his sculptors would refine the details of the pirates, townsfolk, and animals that populate the various scenes until the personalities, humor, and emotions that Davis conveyed on the page became clear in the plaster, clay, and other materials they used. This striving for believability, in addition to the audio-animatronic technology that would eventually allow the characters to come to life, contributed greatly to guests' willingness to suspend disbelief as they became more deeply immersed within the fantasy world the Imagineers created.

In addition to the four new attractions created while working on the 1964-1965 New York World's Fair, Walt discovered a great deal of human capital, including Alice Davis, wife of animator-turned-Imagineer Marc Davis, who dressed the many dolls of "it's a small world" based on the designs of Mary Blair. Delighted with her work on his hit New York attraction, Walt requested that she costume his pirates and the other inhabitants of the Caribbean town. Her ingenuity and experience born from time spent working on Small World helped her meet the challenges of fitting elaborately designed clothing over audio-animatronic characters that were often constructed of little more than tube and wire, and subject to constant movement which led to considerable wear and tear.

The audio-animatronic characters themselves would be designed by a team led by Wathel Rogers, yet another animator turned Imagineer. Co-founder of Imagineering's model shop, he would eventually go on to develop the audio-animatronic birds for the Enchanted Tiki Room and, with the assistance of a newly formed division of Imagineering named MAPO (inspired by the funding source that made its creation possible, *Mary Poppins*), the many complex characters for Pirates of the Caribbean. Their efforts would serve to further immerse guests within the illusion of life as the programmed synchronized movements of their creations mimicked human behavior in ways both subtle and meticulous.

In 1966, when models alone could no longer suggest the scope of the attraction, a full-scale mockup of the auction sequence was constructed as a warehouse walk-through for Walt and his Imagineers. Unfortunately, this sequence would be the only one that Walt lived to see and approve.

Though he would tell most associates that his recent health concerns were due to an old polo injury, Walt and his family knew better. A smoker for nearly half a century, Walt was hospitalized on November 2, 1966, for the removal of a portion of his left lung. Returning to the studio on November 21, the same day he was discharged, Walt discussed a potential pre-Christmas opening of Pirates with his staff, but insisted it be completely ready before its debut even be considered. On December 5, he was readmitted to the hospital for a tumor that had been discovered during his previous visit. He would never again leave.

Nearly six months prior to Walt's death, New Orleans Square would open, serving as the eventual port of call for the Pirates of the Caribbean and all who would eventually set sail with them. Work on the attraction would continue into the new year, with Imagineering obsessing over every detail until they were confident in their belief that it appeared as Walt would have wanted—but also, in a trend that would continue for the next several years, with a listlessness when it came to the idea of moving forward without their supremely confident leader.

Finally, in the spring of 1967, the pirates took their maiden voyage. Following a ceremony in New Orleans Square that featured the Sailing Ship *Columbia* and a cast of pirates led by Disneyland personality Wally Boag, the attraction would prove an instant and enduring classic, with its perfect synthesis of whimsical storytelling, world building, and technical wizardry.

The death of Walt Disney would leave a feeling of uncertainty as to the direction of the future of the studio's entertainment empire, and the theme park division was in no way immune from the lingering hesitancy. Despite the clear success of the ride in Disneyland, Pirates of the Caribbean was not originally planned for inclusion in what would become Walt Disney World, chiefly due to the hefty price tag of the attraction and the need to keep the new park within budget.

Further justification was made that as Florida itself was so close to the actual Caribbean, the people who lived there would not be as engaged with a whimsical experience of buccaneers and pirates who were already so much a part of their culture. Instead, the Imagineers would devote their creative energies to a wholly new experience named Western River Expedition. Designed by Marc Davis, this water ride would be themed to cowboys and Indians and feature scenes including a stagecoach holdup, saloon show, bank robbery, and other iconic stops through the American West.

However, when Walt Disney World opened without Pirates, which in just four years had become as much a part of the Disneyland experience as Main Street, U.S.A., Sleeping Beauty Castle, and Peter Pan's Flight, visitors were appalled by the oversight. Of course, many had visited Disneyland in its nearly two decades of operation, or had heard of the still relatively new attraction from family and friends on the West Coast, but countless others had seen its development chronicled in their living rooms on *Walt Disney's Wonderful World of Color.* The decision was soon made to scrap Western River Expedition for a second Pirates.

With no New Orleans Square in Orlando, the Walt Disney World version of Pirates would find its home in Adventureland, within the walls of Castillo del Morro, a replica of an old Spanish fortress. Budget constraints and a rush to deliver the attraction to satisfy anxious guests would prevent Marc Davis and other Imagineers from improving on the original incarnation of the ride, despite the wisdom they had gained in hindsight and the technological innovations that had become available to them in the intervening years, but they were not without new ideas. Jason Surrell noted:

> One proposed scene would have bridged the narrative gap between the pirates in their "yo-ho" heyday and the grisly fate awaiting them in their haunted grottoes, but alas, Marc's Island of Lost Souls never made it off his drawing board.

The death of Walt Disney would cast a shadow over the company he founded for well over a decade, but efforts to step outside that shadow would perhaps be most evident in Disney's theme park division. After Walt's older brother Roy helped open Walt Disney World in the fall of 1971, with Epcot Center following eleven years later, the Imagineers would soon see if the Disney storytelling magic could translate into another language with the opening of Tokyo Disneyland, their first attempt at an international park, in April 1983. At this point, the Imagineering team was experiencing a transitional period, with Walt's original team of hand-picked talent reaching retirement age and new talent eager to prove themselves.

Fortunately, in the Japanese they had an audience eager for the Disney experience, demanding near replicas of iconic attractions such as Cinderella Castle, Peter Pan's Flight, and Pirates of the Caribbean. The opportunity to bring these familiar concepts to Tokyo would prove an invaluable learning experience for the new crop of Imagineers. The swashbuckling adventure would once again find its home in Adventureland, with a bit of the French Quarter inserted into the wild of the jungle.

While even the popular Blue Bayou restaurant of the Anaheim original was preserved, there are minor variations, but of course the most notable difference would be the use of the Japanese language mixed in with the predominantly English dialogue used throughout the ride. Hoping nothing would be lost in translation, Xavier Atencio recalled in a 1984 episode of *The Disney Family Album* how the ghostly pirate voice that warns passengers "Dead men tell no tales" has no equivalent in Japanese. "We had to come up with something along the lines of, 'If you're not careful, you will not pass this way again," he said.

As it had for Walt Disney World and Disneyland before it, Tokyo's take on the unscrupulous scoundrels that once sailed the Caribbean would prove an instant success and a confidence boost.

In 1984, with the company now under the leadership of Frank Wells and Michael Eisner, a site outside of Paris was selected for what would initially be known as Euro Disney Resort and later Disneyland Paris. Disney would find that unlike the Japanese, the French wanted more than mere replicas of perennially popular American rides and attractions. This allowed Imagineers to revisit their designs from the ground up, and in the case of Pirates of the Caribbean, look at ways to correct perceived flaws in both story design and technology that had troubled them for the better part of two decades.

An imposing fortress would be the setting of Paris' version of the attraction, tucked deep within Adventureland. Across a lagoon, guests can see Captain Hook's *Jolly Roger* moored with the foreboding sight of Skull Rock also visible in the distance, further immersing guests in the visual language of pirates.

These visual elements were also crucial to the story design, as Imagineers were interested in presenting something that not only drew from the best of the Anaheim original, but took advantage of recent innovations in audio-animatronics and special effects and could communicate fluently with new and modern audiences, regardless of their language. To preserve the two drops of the original Disneyland version despite the high water table of the French locale, the designers constructed the show building upward, rather than digging into the ground.

Interestingly, as design of the attraction progressed, the Imagineers decided to present many of the popular dark ride's most familiar elements almost in reverse. As guests ascend through the bowels of the old Spanish fortress, they witness a battle off in the distance. Once inside, silhouettes of soldiers doing battle with attacking pirates give way to the iconic vignette of imprisoned pirates attempting to coax a key from a reluctant four-legged jailer.

The care taken to translate the appeal of this classic Disney dark ride for new audiences would elevate its storytelling. Guests find that they have floated into the heat of battle and an errant cannonball has flooded the fortress, creating a pathway for their boats through the prison. The boats continue through the fortress, only to rush into the harbor, into the middle of yet another battle, as the besieged fortress attempts to repel cannon fire from a pirate ship. Jason Surrell explains:

> Unlike the three previous incarnations of the attraction, this time, the guests are not invisible to the story's characters; the buccaneers actually see them and target their bateaux with cannon fire, making the scene more immersive than its predecessors.

Passengers continue forward through the burning town and watch dueling audio-animatronic buccaneers before an explosion in the town's arsenal, set ablaze from all of the cannon fire, sends them downward in a climactic rush, with a souvenir photo marking the descent into oblivion. Passing the classic grotto scenes of skeletal pirates protecting their plunder that date back to the Anaheim original, guests see the consequences of a life spent in such villainous pursuits.

In 2003, Walt Disney Pictures released *Pirates of the Caribbean: The Curse of the Black Pearl*, the first in a series of box-office hits based on the long popular attraction. Suddenly new generations of fans were arguably more familiar with the film than with the dark ride itself, and it was up to the Imagineers to reconcile this incongruity. Meet and greets and shows featuring new characters like Captain Jack Sparrow were easy enough to offer outside of the attraction, but could the Imagineers successfully mix elements of the new film with the original dark ride created so many years before?

Everything crafted by Disney's Imagineers is driven by story. By this time, Disney park guests around the world had a passion for Pirates of the Caribbean and its colorful cast of audio-animatronic characters. Rather than bow to fan service and randomly insert popular characters into scenes, in the parks where the film and original attraction have blended, the cinematic characters have become part of the existing story, accommodating purists and satisfying those new to the ride through the film. Now, Captain Barbossa leads the pirate assault on the fortress and continues his vendetta against Jack Sparrow, who is seen by passengers throughout the ride in search of treasure. Due in no small part to the staying power of its inspiration, the atmosphere and adventure of the film series has been fused effectively into the classic dark ride. Passages from the film's score are used alongside the classic audio tracks and the cast of the film recorded new dialogue to further immerse guests within the newly blended worlds.

It was a quarter century between the opening of Pirates of the Caribbean at Disneyland and the third version of the classic dark ride to set sail at Disneyland Paris. Nearly as much time would pass before the fourth incarnation would debut at Shanghai Disneyland in the summer of 2016, and given its reception, many would argue it was worth the wait.

The first version to post-date the popular series of films inspired by the original dark ride, Pirates of the Caribbean: Battle for the Sunken Treasure pulls its inspiration from the silver screen, like the classic Disneyland dark rides of old. Jettisoning even the cheerful sea chanty "Yo Ho (A Pirate's Life for Me)" in favor of elements from the film's score, we find Captain Jack Sparrow in an all-new adventure. Dare we join him beneath the depths of the sea and face the dangerous Kraken and the even more lethal Davey Jones, all in the hope of helping Jack acquire his gold?

The design work of Disney's Imagineers set a new standard with their latest pirate adventure. Using the same digital effects that have come to revolutionize the movie-going experience, passengers are made to feel as if their boats are diving countless fathoms beneath the sea to explore shipwrecks and narrowly evade sea monsters and burst back to the surface in the midst of a raging pirate battle.

There are references to the classic dark ride, but the experience is at its best when it is breaking new ground. And with nearly fifty years since the premiere of the original Anaheim attraction, there was ample opportunity to do so in Shanghai. Featuring the latest in audio-animatronic technology and lighting effects, particularly in one jaw-dropping sequence involving Captain Jack Sparrow early in the adventure, the film-based characters are brought to life with state-of-the-art design.

However, what is perhaps even more significant to this particular update is the ride mechanism itself. In Disney's early days of water ride design and its partnership with Arrow Development on attractions such as "it's a small world" and the original Pirates of the Caribbean, water would flow through the canal designed for the ride and the speed of the boats would vary depending on the number of passengers, their size, weight, and other factors. Boats would bump into each other and the timing of attraction scenes would sometimes prove difficult to control. Shanghai Disneyland's updated ride system features boats that can travel forward, backward— even sideways. The modified system can control the pacing of the boats and match elements of the attraction to them. Additionally, each boat can carry up to thirty passengers and though seemingly unguided, are tracked in such a way that the Imagineers were better able to control what guests see, and when they see it. Also, since energy is needed only to move the boats, rather than pumps being used to "move" the water, as was the case with previous versions of Pirates, the attraction is more energy efficient.

Happy Haunts

More than half a century ago, Walt Disney's original plans for a pirate-themed attraction involved a modest walk-through wax museum, albeit with a Disney twist. Generations of theme park guests in the decades since then are no doubt grateful Walt was an ambitious man. Similar ambitions led to a desire to include a haunted house in his plans for what would eventually become Disneyland. As far back as 1951, long before his dreams of a theme park would firmly take root in Anaheim, Walt was considering a "Mickey Mouse Park" across the street from his Burbank studio. The genesis of Disneyland, this small park would include an homage to the classic American Main Street, a Western village, a working farm, railroad, carnival, Disney characters, and other attractions. Walt assigned Harper Goff to render a series of conceptual designs, one of the earliest of which included a dilapidated Victorian mansion on a hill overlooking a cemetery.

Walt's evolving plans would rapidly outgrow the limited space available to him in Burbank. Two years later a parcel of land over an hour south of the studio in Anaheim was selected for the newly named Disneyland. Before the likes of Marc Davis and Claude Coats would join the ranks of artists and designers recruited from within the Disney studios to help him realize his dream, Walt founded Walt Disney, Inc., soon to be renamed WED Enterprises, and these talented individuals would form the basis of what would eventually become known as Walt Disney Imagineering.

Artists and storymen in their own right, these early Imagineers were tasked with bringing the classic Disney stories to three-dimensional life. Using their background in animation, they would storyboard the layout of the theme park's various settings and attractions just as they would scenes from the films that inspired them.

Harper Goff's early take on an eerie haunted house at the end of a typical turn-of-the-century Main Street was eventually shelved as the shape of Disney's first theme park solidified. Along with the proposed farm and carnival concepts, plans for a haunted house had given way, at least temporarily, to a series of themed "lands," and on a midsummer day in 1955, Disneyland would at last open as the embodiment of Walt's greatest dream. In his magical new world of yesterday, tomorrow, and fantasy, he invited guests to create connections with his exciting new theme park attractions in the same way he had been doing for decades with his animated features.

In the late 1950s, as the park's early success allowed for the addition of three major attractions that would close out the decade, Walt would look back to the early designs for a haunted house to serve as a companion attraction for his newly conceived New Orleans Square. As was the case with Pirates of the Caribbean, he would continue to pull trusted talent from the ranks of his animators and turn them into Imagineers. Walt assigned writer and art director Ken Anderson, who had already done design work on other popular dark rides, such as Snow White's Scary Adventures and Mr. Toad's Wild Ride, to pick up where planning had left off years before, dusting off Harper Goff's sketches of a haunted house.

As New Orleans Square was to border Frontierland, Anderson's research steered him toward the elegant southern plantation homes common to antebellum Louisiana. The mansion's final design would in fact more closely resemble a mid-19th century mansion found in Baltimore, Maryland, an opulent forty-eight room mansion on twenty-six acres of land once owned by the Garrett family, who made its fortune in the railroad industry. The Garrett mansion was left to Johns Hopkins University and is now open to the public as the Evergreen Museum and Library.

Walt decided that Goff's work would need considerably more than a dusting-off. He insisted that the ghostly abode be in keeping with the pristine nature of the rest of his park when he famously declared: "Let the ghosts take care of the inside and we'll take care of the outside." Neither the ramshackle look of Goff's early design nor Anderson's updated sketch framed by foreboding trees and a decaying plantation house nearly engulfed by overgrown landscaping found favor with Walt.

While Walt Disney would busy himself talking up the latest expansion plans for his theme park, on one vacation to England going so far as to suggest to local media that he had come to search castles and manor homes throughout the British countryside for ghosts who might be in need of a new home to haunt after the London Blitz, Ken Anderson set about designing the interior of their lodgings.

Much like early concepts for the neighboring pirate attraction, Disney's haunted house was initially conceived of as walk-through experience, and Anderson's first approach would reflect this. A series of sketched vignettes dated to 1957 take guests on a tour of the home of an old sea captain who had disappeared under mysterious circumstances many years before. With a maid or butler character as their guide, visitors would gather in a portrait gallery before descending to a lower level where the tour began.

As they were led deeper into the mansion, guests would learn about its one-time owner, Captain Gore, who had left his former life behind to retire a wealthy man in a seaside town and took a pretty young bride named Priscilla. On the day they were to be wed, his curious bride-to-be found a locked sea chest in the mansion's attic, and on forcing it open, discovered the dark secrets of the captain's past life as a ruthless pirate. Enraged that his long-kept secret might be revealed by this foolish young girl, the pirate threw her out the window to her doom. Priscilla, in turn, would come back from beyond the grave, relentlessly tormenting Captain Gore until he ended his own life, choosing to hang himself from the rafters in the mansion's attic. As guests left the mansion, they would walk by an old well, with bubbles rising to the surface of the murky red water offering a clue to Priscilla's final resting place.

Anderson's second treatment of the haunted house's backstory would relate the history of Bloodmere Manor, a southern estate home that had been relocated to Disneyland. Members of the Blood family had all met with violent deaths and their ghosts remained behind to reside in their ancestral home. According to Anderson's story, though Disney's dedicated staff labored daily to restore the home to its original splendor, their work would be undone nightly by the mischievous spirits.

Several months later, in August 1957, a more light-hearted take would invite guests to witness a spirited wedding celebration and featured Walt Disney himself as narrator.

By fall of the same year, Anderson began considering an approach that, like the Fantasyland dark rides, would take advantage of one of Disney's own animated gems, the second half of the 1949 package feature *The Adventures of Ichabod and Mr. Toad*. In this version of the attraction, the arrival of the Headless Horseman, vengeful villain of Washington Irving's "The Legend of Sleepy Hollow," in the mansion's courtyard would signal the start of a wedding party where guests would encounter Dracula, Frankenstein's Monster, and other creatures. Perhaps a bit leery of what she is about to marry into, the bride-to-be leaves her groom at the altar and amid the ensuing chaos, guests escape through a secret passage hidden in a fireplace.

Work would progress for more than a year with this story treatment inspiring the Imagineers. By the end of 1959, many of Anderson's earlier concepts would re-emerge as story elements to spark their creativity.

Additional talent was brought on board by Walt from his animation team to help move the project forward, including Rolly Crump and Yale Gracey. Crump's hobbies of magic and sculpture made him a natural fit for attraction design, and Gracey's interest in model-making and mechanics made them a perfect pair as the effects and illusions within the mansion began to take shape. This particularly fruitful period saw Disney's first use of the Pepper's Ghost effect, which would eventually yield extraordinary results in the celebration scene in the mansion's grand hall, and in the development of disquieting marble busts that seemed to follow an observer's every move.

Crump and Gracey created a mock-up of the attraction using Anderson's designs, which at this point had also been informed by a visit he had paid to the Winchester Mystery

House in San Jose, California. Sarah Winchester, widow of the inventor of the namesake rifle, had consulted a spiritualist on how best to break a curse placed on her family by the spirits of those slain by her husband's creation and spent thirty-eight years supervising the construction a labyrinthine mansion, with staircases and doors that led to nowhere and other design features to help prevent the restless spirits from finding her.

The latest mock-up featured the return of the ghostly sea captain and his ill-fated wife who came back to haunt him, but when Disneyland's management saw it play out, they considered the effect too complicated to stage, especially for a walk-through attraction. Walt, too, remained unsatisfied with the still ramshackle appearance of the haunted house, and as park capacity was becoming an increasing concern, was equally unsettled by the slow and unpredictable pace of a walk-through.

In 1961, ground would break on New Orleans Square, which the progress-plagued haunted house would eventually call home alongside Pirates of the Caribbean. Employees passed out advertisements at Disneyland's main entrance hinting at a 1963 opening for the newly named Haunted Mansion, and though Imagineers did their best, by the time 1963 arrived, all that guests could experience was the puzzling promise of the mansion's exterior. Though its designers would take Walt's directive to "take care of the outside" to heart, it would otherwise resemble the original designs of Ken Anderson and Sam McKim, who had taken Anderson's early sketch and painted it years earlier.

Inside the mansion was another matter. Completely empty within, the mansion would remain vacant, intriguing curious park goers as the Imagineers turned their attention to the more pressing matter of the 1964-1965 New York World's Fair. While most of the department's focus shifted eastward, a young writer and Imagineer by the name of Marty Sklar helped craft a clever tease to promote the new attraction inspired by comments made by Walt during the London trip when he first began actively promoting a haunted house attraction years before:

> Notice! All Ghosts And Restless Spirits. Post-lifetime leases are Now available in this HAUNTED MANSION. Don't be left out in the sunshine! Enjoy active retirement

in this country club atmosphere—the fashionable address for famous ghosts, ghosts trying to make a name for themselves and ghosts afraid to live by themselves! Leases include license to scare the daylights out of guests visiting the Portrait Gallery, Museum of the Supernatural, graveyard and other happy haunting grounds. For reservations send resume of past experience to: Ghost Relations Dept. Disneyland. Please! Do not apply in person.

Ken Anderson shifted his focus back to animation when the project was put on the back burner yet again, and Marc Davis and Claude Coats were assigned by Walt to work on the mansion in the summer of 1964. As they had for Pirates of the Caribbean, Coats would focus on the mansion's interior and set design, while Davis would rework the attraction's story elements and give life to the spooks and specters within.

Soon enough, they would be joined by Xavier Atencio, who had written the script for Pirates of the Caribbean and seemed an ideal choice for the equally original Haunted Mansion.

Work would continue with hundreds of design ideas being developed over the next two-and-a-half years, but as it had for so many aspects of the company that bore his name, Walt Disney's death on December 15, 1966, would send development of the Haunted Mansion into chaos and lead to serious creative differences between its most prominent and revered designers. Sam McKim, one of the mansion's earliest contributors, understood exactly what was going on:

> In the early days, everybody was trying to please Walt. He was the conductor of the orchestra. We all worked with each other; the good ideas that someone came up with, you tried to be faithful to those. Where necessary, you added your own little bit, but the ultimate decision was with Walt. After his death, his key lieutenants did their best to keep that Disney teamwork and spirit intact.

Though he would not live to see the end result of their collaborative efforts, Walt knew that in pairing Marc Davis and Claude Coats to develop Pirates of the Caribbean, they would combine their unique talents to create something remarkable, and he clearly felt the same when he teamed them up once again for the Haunted Mansion. However, especially now with Walt no longer in the picture to cast a deciding vote, both of these gifted artists were confident enough in their own abilities to feel that they should be given a longer leash creatively and more autonomy over this new assignment. Davis, a character and storyman, felt that the attraction should include gags and be more lighthearted, as ghosts would be featured by default. Coats, who was responsible for some of the more chilling elements of Snow White's Scary Adventures and Mr. Toad's Wild Ride, felt the attraction begged to be scary.

Dick Irvine, executive vice president of Imagineering, would ultimately side with Davis, but the end result would turn out to be something of a combination of disparate tastes. Davis' story treatment introduced an ethereal "Ghost Host," and though this disembodied character would welcome guests into the mansion, the early portion of the experience sets a somewhat sinister mood. It is not until guests have traveled deeper within the mansion that they begin to see Davis' comical character designs.

As he had for Pirates of the Caribbean, which much like the Haunted Mansion was shaping up to be less a linear story than a series of loosely connected scenes with arguably questionable subject matter, Xavier Atencio understood that it could all be brought together with the right musical elements. Partnering this time with studio composer Buddy Baker, he would pen "Grim Grinning Ghosts" to flow perfectly through the entire attraction, with no beginning or end. To preserve continuity, the song's melody would be resurrected in various forms throughout the experience, whether as a morbid funeral dirge or an all-stops-pulled-out jazzy rendition in the mansion's graveyard.

Though the song and its melody would provide the connective tissue throughout the various vignettes, the task of crafting a cohesive narrative around the contrasting elements created by Davis and Coats remained. Delays over the mansion's direction and its relegation to an afterthought during the rush to meet deadlines for the World's Fair would turn out to be something of a blessing, as it created a wholly new way for guests to experience the attraction.

To accommodate the massive crowds at the New York World's Fair, Disney's design team had developed an endless transit system dubbed the PeopleMover that was put to use for Ford's Magic Skyway. Later, considering the many innovations learned at the fair that could be applied back at Anaheim, Imagineer Bob Gurr developed a ride system he would call the omnimover, using the PeopleMover as his starting point. Passengers would step from a moving conveyor belt into a tracked vehicle that was moving at the same speed. The vehicles, each one of many in a seemingly endless loop, could tilt, swivel, and turn to direct the attention of a passenger and control sight lines toward whatever the story required, giving Imagineers as much control over the ride experience as a director has with a camera.

The omnimover was introduced in Tomorrowland's Adventure Thru Inner Space. Its potential benefits for both story direction and ride capacity proved the perfect solution for the inchoate mansion, after a coat of black paint and the designation of "Doom Buggy." The walk-through attraction had become a ride.

While the switch from a slow-paced walk-through attraction to a more traditional dark ride had its immediate advantages, it did necessitate rethinking some of the scenes and effects, which had been designed for stationary guests. Ultimately, it gave Atencio the means to marry the contrasting design elements presented by Coats and Davis, matching their characters and settings to the ghoulish illusions crafted by Gracey and Crump with the music penned by Baker and Atencio himself into a workable story.

The self-same restless spirits that Walt had scoured the British countryside for many years earlier and that Marty Sklar would lure with an engraved invitation would serve as a loose backstory for the Haunted Mansion. Though this dark ride may not have as coherent a narrative as Peter Pan's Flight or Pinocchio's Daring Journey, which owe their inspiration to their animated source material, there is absolutely a story being told as guests move through the mansion, and it is one that the Imagineers would continue to refine in the years to come.

After being ushered inside by a human servant, we're welcomed into the macabre mansion by an unseen host, who immediately senses our apprehension as he hints at the curiosities within the suddenly crowded foyer. The seemingly innocent portraits on the walls gradually take on a more sinister appearance and at the same time the room itself appears to begin stretching. This conceals the fact that we're being lowered by an elevator to the show building, while the Ghost Host, voiced by Paul Frees, who had also narrated the Pirates of the Caribbean, relates the story of his own unfortunate demise and a flash of lightning reveals his lifeless body hanging from the rafters above, much like Ken Anderson's early concepts for Captain Gore. He then challenges us to find our way out of the dark and doorless room.

Now exploring a hallway lined with windows on one side and portraits on the other, we hear that the mansion plays host to spirits who have retired. Moving onward, we notice that these portraits also transform. Tucked into a wall are the busts of two dour-looking individuals whose stern gaze mysteriously seems to follow us as we move toward our waiting Doom Buggies.

Stepping onto a moving walkway, we board the black ride vehicle. A suit of armor appears to have been jostled by our arrival. We find ourselves peering down an endless corridor where a candelabra floats in midair, lighting the way for one of the mansion's many disembodied residents. The procession of Doom Buggies continues through the mansion's conservatory, where it would appear someone may have been laid to rest prematurely, as two emaciated hands desperately try to raise the heavy lid of their coffin. It is here for the first time that we also see a raven, which at one point was in consideration as the mansion's host, before the Imagineers decided that it was too small and too difficult for guests to focus their attention on.

Passing next through a corridor of doors, we hear relentless pounding from the other side. Doorknobs twist and knockers knock by themselves as eyes glare at us from the sinister-looking wallpaper. Just before turning a corner, we pass a ghoulishly ornate grandfather clock, its hands spinning rapidly as they ceaselessly strike thirteen.

At this point, the deceased denizens of the mansion have grown increasingly restless and we soon see why as the Doom Buggies gather around a seance circle led by Madame Leota, herself a spirit within a crystal ball, who is actively summoning them from somewhere beyond. Musical instruments float in the air, sounding off in response to her pleas.

One of the many early illusions created for the attraction by Crump and Gracey, this other-worldly effect features additional talent in the presence of Leota Toombs, an Imagineer whose face is used to bring her kindred spirit to life. Leota's incantations are voiced by veteran Disney voice actress Eleanor Audley, known for her memorable work as Cinderella's wicked stepmother and Maleficent.

It would seem Leota's charms prove successful as the Doom Buggies next overlook a grand hall. From the balcony above, we witness the mansion's assorted residents brought together for a swinging wake.

Ghosts appear and disappear throughout the scene as lightning rages outside. Some gather at a dining room table while others hang from a chandelier. As we continue farther through the hall, "Grim Grinning Ghosts" is played by a ghostly organist as couples dance the waltz. This sequence also owes itself to Crump and Gracey's early tinkering and features an extraordinarily sophisticated use of the Pepper's Ghost effect, through which we see objects through a plate of glass positioned at an angle and objects reflected off the glass at the same time. Imagineers carefully placed the audio-animatronic ghost figures to match the physical props so they appear and disappear as the lighting is manipulated.

The Doom Buggies continue into the attic, dusty and forgotten with time, though for those aware of the earliest concepts for this dark ride, not completely removed from memory. The resting place of countless family heirlooms, the attic is also home to the mansion's unfortunate bride, whose mournful promise of "Here comes the bride" elicits both sorrow and terror.

Then, as if thrown from the attic window, the Doom Buggies turn downward. As the melody of "Grim Grinning Ghosts" quickens its pace and spirits rise up in the distance, a terrified caretaker sees us as we pass into the mansion's graveyard.

The attraction's theme takes on a jazzy feel with apparitions tapping out the melody over headstones using bones and other makeshift instruments. A quintet of singing busts joins in for a chorus as ghosts continue to come out to socialize. Thurl Ravenscroft, who had provided voices for a number of Disneyland attractions, including the Enchanted Tiki Room and Pirates of the Caribbean, is heard singing lead vocals.

We are joined once more by the Ghost Host who warns us to beware of hitch-hiking ghosts as we enter the mansion's crypt. Sure enough, as the Doom Buggy passes a wall of large mirrors, it has taken on an extra passenger: one of three ghosts has decided to try and follow us home.

Stepping off the Doom Buggy back onto the moving platform, we see one final spirit, in the form of the Bride, now in a much smaller form, urging guests to "make final arrangements now," as she is certain we will return.

It had been six years since the exterior of the Haunted Mansion was built and longer still since Walt Disney first began enticing Disneyland guests with talk of his version of a spook house attraction, so when the attraction finally opened in August 1969, anticipation was considerable—enough so that a single day attendance record was set and the dark ride, with no legacy film having inspired it, became an instant hit that would continue to delight Disneyland guests for decades to come. Unlike any other Disney dark ride before it, guests were transported into an experience with their own private host. The Doom Buggies were designed in such a way that the attraction's Ghost Host, though disembodied, can be heard from each of them individually, as if the occupant of that vehicle alone is the mansion's potential one-thousandth happy haunt. The personal experience created by the effective use of ride narration is as significant an enhancement in story immersion as the use of the Doom Buggies to guide the guests' line of site.

The enthusiasm for this attraction would not be limited to Anaheim for long, as planning for Walt Disney World in Orlando called for its own take on the Haunted Mansion. When development of the original was solidified, Imagineers began building two of everything for the attraction's interior.

The exterior was another matter. With the bicentennial of the United States following just a few short years after Walt Disney World's planned 1971 opening, Imagineers turned to an abandoned Disneyland concept for Liberty Street that Walt had considered some years earlier as a way for guests to appreciate the significance of their country's heritage, giving rise to Liberty Square. This time, rather than a stately southern manor house, a Dutch Gothic-style mansion, typical of the sort found in New York's Hudson River Valley, was used, blending seamlessly with the nearby Hall of Presidents, Liberty Tree Tavern, and the other immersive elements in the area.

The Haunted Mansion would be as popular with guests of Disney's Orlando theme park as it had been when it opened in Anaheim two years earlier. When the Imagineers began to consider ideas for Tokyo Disneyland, their first venture outside of the United States, it seemed certain that they would recycle a number of their most celebrated attractions. The first international version of the mansion would open with Tokyo Disneyland's Fantasyland in April 1983 as a nearly identical replica of the Orlando attraction. Its European design influence lent itself to the mansion's Fantasyland setting, with the only significant difference being the addition of a pair of winged beasts that sit as stewards over its front gate.

For nearly fifteen years and now in three Disney parks, the Haunted Mansion would delight audiences with its mix of enchanting effects, witty gags, and an unforgettable theme song. Less than a decade after the Haunted Mansion opened in Tokyo, Imagineers would be tasked with creating an entirely new take on the classic attraction, dubbed Phantom Manor. The real chills come later (in chapter 7).

The enduring appeal of Pirates of the Caribbean and the Haunted Mansion is testament not just to Walt Disney's insight into what sort of attractions spark something within us, but to the roster of talented men and women he assembled in the years leading up to Disneyland and its aftermath. Their continued success after his death is due in no small part to how the attraction's designers managed to project a sense of awe and wonder—both from the characters and the guests experiencing it—through every aspect of the dark ride's design, from their setting and mood to the effects, costumes, and story that help invest us in their imagined creations. The fear, wonder, and even bemusement that we feel as passengers traveling through these attractions is enhanced when similar feelings are expressed by the Ghost Host or to a lesser extent in the warnings of the pirates heard as we begin our trip into the treacherous waters of the Caribbean. The world they have built for us as park visitors becomes more realistic as a result.

CHAPTER FIVE

Go East, Old Man

At the youthful age of twenty-one, a nearly bankrupt Walt Disney moved to California with little more than his suitcase and the hopes of becoming a director. Driven by ambition, dreams, and desperation to succeed, he would eventually build a creative empire enjoyed by generations of people around the world.

By the mid-1960s, he could very easily have settled into retirement, with a resumé that would have satisfied most anyone: from the creation of Mickey Mouse and his assorted animated friends and the staggering success of *Snow White and the Seven Dwarfs* and the many television programs and feature films that followed, to the technical innovations of his studio and the way Disneyland redefined the amusement park industry.

Of course Walt did not create his empire single-handedly. Before his studio played host to a roster of so many gifted animators and Imagineers, before writers, actors, and voice artists gave life to his animated characters, and before Disneyland sold its first turkey leg, Walt's closest and most devoted partner was his brother Roy.

While Walt handled the creative interests of their partnership, Roy tackled the finances, and even after the extraordinary success of Disneyland, Walt's ambitious planning did not end. Progress was second nature to him and the opportunities presented by the recent New York World's Fair were unmistakably encouraging. According to Marty Sklar, Walt wanted "to see if his kind of entertainment would appeal to the more sophisticated eastern audience—'sophisticated' in that that's where the nation's leaders, the decision-makers were based." Leaders or not, by the time it ended its two-year run in Flushing Meadows, "47 million attendees, or 91% of the fair's total guests, had seen at least one of Disney's four attractions."

In early 1963, Walt convened a select group of his executives and instructed them to begin buying land in Florida for a new park. He wanted far more land than he had secured in Anaheim because he had long regretted how spoiled the area surrounding Disneyland had become in the wake of its success by opportunists intent on cashing in on their proximity to Disneyland. Once his executives found a suitable location, they began scooping up thousands of acres of land under various corporate names with no link back to Walt Disney. But a company with a leader as high profile as theirs could only keep its plans secret for so long, and on November 15, 1965, Walt finally revealed his intentions during a press conference at Orlando's Cherry Plaza Hotel with his brother Roy and Florida governor Haydon Burns in attendance.

Never one to simply repeat past successes, Walt Disney had resisted the opportunity to create a second Disneyland in the years after his inaugural park opened to such widespread acclaim. It was only as the talents of his team of Imagineers matured that his vision for something far grander than another theme park began to gel. Yes, there would be another park, originally planned to be five times the size of the Anaheim original, but it would serve as a way to entice guests to experience his greater goal and the heart of everything he had planned for Florida: the creation of a new type of city that would be a "showcase to the world for the ingenuity and imagination of American free enterprise." Though Walt's main motivation for his Florida project may have been its potential for helping him realize his dream of an experimental "City of Tomorrow," his untimely passing and the vague directions he left behind of exactly just what that would entail left that particular dream largely unrealized.

Still, on October 25, 1971, after clearing over 27,000 acres and spending $400 million on construction, Walt Disney World would officially open, with Roy Disney on hand to celebrate his brother's last great vision.

The blessing of size coupled with nearly two decades of experience gave Imagineers the opportunity to revisit many of the classic Disneyland dark rides for East Coast audiences, allowing them to invest more time in theming and in some cases lengthen attractions. And with the eventuality of four parks, entirely new worlds and experiences would be made available to guests in the years to come, from lost favorites like Horizons and Maelstrom in Epcot to enduring classics like Space Mountain in the Magic Kingdom. Much like its original inspiration in Anaheim, it has become clear that Walt Disney World will never be complete as long as there is imagination left in the world.

Walt Disney World's Dark Rides

Though Walt would not live to see its completion, Walt Disney World was conceived with the same vision and commitment to storytelling as Disneyland had been nearly two decades earlier. It would be a new world that at once allowed guests to look forward and backward in time and to discover new and previously unimagined realms.

Over the course of its nearly half century of existence, the designers of Walt Disney World have been able to not only realize the many concepts of yesterday, tomorrow, and fantasy first explored by the company's founder in Disneyland so many years earlier in their countless inventive dark rides and the immersive settings meant to draw guests into their creations, but they have in many ways surpassed his vision, developing new content with collaborators such as George Lucas and James Cameron, and thereby creating an even larger canvas on which the dreams of their guests might play out.

The Haunted Mansion
October 1, 1971

Many of the ride elements for this mansion were constructed at the same time as those at Disneyland, but Walt Disney World's version of the attraction is different in numerous respects. Located in the Liberty Square section of the Magic

Kingdom, the most striking difference is its gothic design, inspired by similar mansions that were constructed in the 18th century in New York's Hudson Valley region.

Taking advantage of the availability of significantly more space, the Orlando mansion introduced an interactive queue in 2011 that features several large crypts, including a watery grave belonging to the sea captain whose portrait graces the mansion's walls, a musical tomb that is believed to belong to the resident organist, and a secret library and series of busts.

We enter through the mansion's foyer, which showcases many curious portraits. Disney World's mansion does not require that we be brought down in an elevator, so to retain the popular effect of the stretching room, the portraits themselves move upward.

As we follow the Ghost Host, those familiar with the spectral proprietor of California's mansion will notice that he has less to say in Orlando, likely because there is not quite as much to draw our attention as we stroll through the hallway.

We step into our Doom Buggies, soon making their way past the portraits lining the walls, which prior to 2007 mimicked the effect of the stern-looking busts with their ever-watchful eyes as seen in Disneyland, but now match the effect of its paintings that change as lightning strikes, as a storm visibly rages through windows on the opposite side of the wall. We then pass through a library, where many books are pulled from their shelves by invisible hands and ladders and chairs move about with no one present. The library scene is unique to the Florida and Tokyo versions of the Haunted Mansion.

We next pass through a music room. Original to the Orlando attraction, this scene was not added to the Disneyland version until 1994. We then begin our ascent up a stairway, which features many different paths, some of which head off in tilted and other perplexing directions, not seen in Anaheim.

Spiders that once crossed the path of guests as they approached the Corridor of Doors were removed from the mansion in 2007 and repurposed for Adventureland's Jungle Cruise attraction.

After taking us past scenes similar to those in the Disneyland mansion, we pass through the mansion's attic.

Until 1994 this scene was the same in both parks, when Orlando's piano player was added to the Anaheim attraction to play an eerie version of "The Wedding March." Some years later, in both U.S. mansions, a new bride was added, who is rumored to have killed her rich husbands for their money. Disney World's finale with the Hitchhiking Ghosts was redone in 2012 with facial recognition technology, and since 2016, guests wearing Magic Bands may even be recognized by name.

Glow-in-the-dark stickers were replaced with fiber-optic stars in Disney World's graveyard scene in 2007, to match the effect of those in Disneyland, and guests pass through trees also similar to those found in Anaheim, but are somewhat obscured and lack the hint of ghoulish faces, as seen in California.

As the ride comes to an end, guests familiar with both American versions of the attraction will notice that Little Leota, a diminutive standing specter with the same face as Madame Leota, is seen just before riders disembark, while in Anaheim, she is spotted as the Doom Buggy makes its way up through the mansion's interior.

Disney World's Ghost Host offers some final instructions and we make our way out of the mansion through a hallway, where we encounter the servant's quarters and a memorial to Bluebeard. Farther on the path is the cemetery and the Memento Mori gift shop. In Disneyland, guests exit the mansion onto the same street they entered, almost as if what they'd just witnessed was a figment of their imagination.

"it's a small world"
October 1, 1971

Though this attraction remains happy and upbeat wherever it is found and shares the same message of global unity as its small boats carry visitors around the world, each version is unique in varying ways. The Goodbye Room in Orlando's version features farewell good wishes written on stylized flowers and personalized farewells for guests with Magic Bands, while in Disneyland, parting phrases are shared on oversized postcards.

Orlando's version of "it's a small world" saw a major refurbishment in 2005 and re-opened with new lighting effects and a loading area that resembles the façade of its Anaheim counterpart.

Peter Pan's Flight
October 3, 1971

Another beneficiary of recent renovation, with a newly themed queue having opened in 2015, Walt Disney World's incarnation of Peter Pan's Flight now begins its experience with a walk through a quiet street in Bloomsbury, the Darling family's London neighborhood, before moving on to a corridor in their home with interactive portraits and a smattering of pixie dust as guests make their way to the family's nursery. Guests then proceed to board their pirate ship and are whisked off to Neverland, which is only marginally different from its original Disneyland incarnation.

Pirates of the Caribbean
December 15, 1973

Like the Haunted Mansion, arguably one of the most influential dark ride attractions ever conceived, the Orlando version of Pirates retains the highly elaborate queue, spectacle, and scale of the Disneyland attraction, though its presence in Disney World was not always a given. Disney Imagineers had initially considered a Western River Expedition, which would carry passengers via boat through scenes of the American Old West. After park guests demanded Pirates, a rush was made to build that attraction instead. The ride's popularity has made it an essential element of the Magic Kingdom since its opening in 1973.

Due to its very high water table, Orlando's version is also absent a second drop and much of the interior of the burning city seen in the Disneyland version was not duplicated. Guests also exit immediately after the scene with Jack Sparrow in the treasure cove, while in Anaheim they remain in their boats until reaching the loading station.

The exterior of the attraction was revamped in 2006 with a new sign for the ride that resembled a ship's mast, its name written in the black sails and a skeleton on duty in the crow's nest. Additionally, Pirate's once prominent barker bird was relocated to the World of Disney Store in Disney Springs.

Spaceship Earth
March 1, 1982

Housed in Epcot's iconic landmark, there have been four different versions of Spaceship Earth since 1982. Guests travel through the eighteen-story interior learning humanity's developments in communication as depicted by animatronic scenes of prehistoric cave paintings, the invention of printing, television, computers, the dawn of the Internet, and beyond. Interactive screens in the ride vehicles allow for a customized version of an animated video that appears at the end of the ride. An end-of-show area has interactive exhibits and games.

Science-fiction author and avid Disney fan Ray Bradbury helped conceive the attraction's original story and also advised on its spherical exterior. With ride narration provided by Judi Dench, Jeremy Irons, Walter Cronkite, and others throughout its operational evolution, guests take a ride through time to witness the key moments in history that make today's methods of communication possible and hint at what's to come.

We begin at the dawn of recorded human history, when cave walls served as a canvas to capture the thoughts of ancient humans, then move on to learn of the development of the alphabet and papyrus before humankind's potential for the dissemination of knowledge exploded with the invention of Gutenberg's printing press. This in turn gave rise to the wonders of the Renaissance, before we rocket forward to more recent times, with newspapers and television sharing information and ideas on a massive scale and computer technology hinting at the prospect of the marvels to come. We can explore these wonders themselves from the comfort of our vehicle, as we fashion our own notion of the future.

Humanity's forward motion as it relates to the technology of communication should move forward continuously, much like

the omnimover track that guides the ride's vehicles, guarantee-
ing endless opportunities for Imagineers to revisit and update
the ride. In fact, it was not until 2007 that they introduced
the interactive elements and allowed non-English speakers to
enjoy its narrative elements with a multi-language option.

Living with the Land
October 1, 1982

This Epcot dark ride shows firsthand how Walt Disney World's
horticulturalists are using new and innovative farming techniques as they work toward sustaining the growing global
population, giving guests a newfound appreciation for where
their food comes from.

Passengers are conveyed on boats through swampland and
other areas not always suited for farming before arriving in a
futuristic and constantly changing greenhouse environment
where crops are grown using the latest in agricultural technology to make farming more environmentally friendly and
efficient. Some of the food grown here is used in restaurants
throughout Disney World.

We begin the ride in a forest scene in the midst of a thunderstorm, learning how the natural forces that help shape the
land can actually appear destructive to casual observers, and
then sail on to a series of biodomes enhanced by lighting and
sound effects: a tropical rainforest, a harsh desert, and the
American prairie.

Along the way, we encounter animatronic figures that
support the attraction's narrative of ecology and technology,
many of which were salvaged from the aborted Western River
Expedition ride.

Our boats then enter a living laboratory where ideas showcasing potential agricultural methods are presented, such as
plants grown hydroponically in sand and in other challenging
environments. We observe ongoing research in five different
sections, including the tropics greenhouse, with crops like
bananas and dragonfruit; the aquacell section, which focuses
on fish farming; a temperate greenhouse; and a string greenhouse, where methods such as vertical growing techniques are

showcased. Along the way we learn that in excess of 30 tons of produce are harvested from The Land each year.

Journey into Imagination with Figment
March 3, 1983

Derived from plans for an attraction from Disneyland's homage to Jules Verne and H.G. Wells in the never-built Discovery Bay, where a bearded scientist had a hobby of breeding dragons, Journey into Imagination was Disney Imagineering's first attempt to explore and explain the creative process in dark ride form.

Another key element of the attraction's initial design manifested when Imagineer Tony Baxter was watching an episode of the television show, *Magnum P.I.* In that episode, Magnum had hidden a goat in Higgins' yard, and the goat had predictably wreaked havoc on the vegetation. When Higgins suggested that a goat was ruining his yard, Magnum replied that it was all just a figment of his imagination. Higgins' response that "Figments don't eat grass!" served as the inspiration for Baxter's new character, named Figment, the purple personification of creativity and imagination.

The journey began with the omnimovers seemingly floating through the clouds. The silhouette of a peculiar blimp crossed with a vacuum cleaner appeared, as the humming and singing of its pilot grew steadily clearer. The pilot of the curious craft, a red-bearded man dressed in a blue suit and top hat, introduced himself as the Dreamfinder. He explained that he uses his strange vehicle, the Dream Mobile, to collect dreams to create all sorts of things. One of those things turned out to be a figment of his imagination named, appropriately enough, Figment.

The ride then showcased a series of rooms, beginning with the Dreamport's Storage Room and the many things inside, including a massive contraption for sorting ideas, a plasma ball, boxed applause, and a birdcage filled with musical notes.

The Art Room featured a giant, mostly white, blank canvas, upon which Dreamfinder and Figment could give shape and form to their imaginations; giant origami animals; and a pot of rainbows.

The Literature Room showed Dreamfinder playing an organ from which he brought forth letters and words, and an over-sized book featuring Edgar Allan Poe's "The Raven" and other suspenseful tales that Figment was clearly wary of. Red eyes and other hints of monsters revealed their presence.

In the Performing Arts Room, while Figment chose his ward-robe behind the scenes, Dreamfinder conducted a laser light spectacular, and in the Science Room, he looked more closely at nature, from the process of plant growth to space exploration.

As the journey reached its end, Dreamfinder and Figment discussed the nature of imagination. Figment sat on a film roll surrounded by screens that showed him using his imagination in several different ways, like flying as if he were a superhero, mountain climbing, sailing, and weightlifting. From behind a movie camera, Dreamfinder advised guests to use their newfound sparks of imagination and visit ImageWorks, the interactive exhibit area and creative playground.

The original version of Journey Into Imagination closed in October 1998 to be loosely re-themed around the *Honey, I Shrunk The Kids* film series.

A year later, the newly conceived attraction opened as Journey into Your Imagination, with guests now taking a tour of the Imagination Institute, only to find themselves as test subjects for the Imagination Scanner, a new device created by Dr. Nigel Channing, portrayed by Monty Python's Eric Idle.

While Figment did make a few scattered cameos in this version of the attraction, Dreamfinder was completely absent. On October 8, 2001, it would close again, reopening in June 2002 as Journey into Imagination with Figment.

With an opening premise similar to its previous incarna-tion, we are once again invited to explore the five sensory labs of the Imagination Institute. This time, much to the chagrin of Dr. Channing, Figment interrupts his introduction and tags along, causing expected mischief as the tour begins in the Sound Lab while Dr. Channing is conducting a hearing test. Figment suggests that listening with your imagination is more important than listening with your ears.

In the Sight Lab, we come upon an eye chart hanging on the wall, but Figment destroys it within seconds and begins singing a version of "One Little Spark" to emphasize the role sight can play in imagination.

In the Smell Lab, Figment enters a slot machine and, taking on the appearance of a skunk, sprays us with a nasty aroma and sends us off with another chorus on using our senses to develop our imagination.

Reluctant to allow things to continue with Figment's constant interruptions, Dr. Channing pauses for a moment and decides to end the tour before we enter the Touch and Taste Labs. Figment feels this is a splendid idea and continues the tour with himself as guide, literally turning things upside down.

Dr. Channing decides that if you can't beat 'em, join 'em, and returns with the realization that imagination works best when it has been set free. Overhead, we see Figment appear in a variety of different scenarios as his imagination has now been sparked and Dr. Channing and Figment sing a final round of "One Little Spark" together before we exit our ride vehicles into the ImageWorks exhibit area.

Splash Mountain
October 2, 1992

With no equivalent to Critter Country in Walt Disney World, Orlando's version of Splash Mountain was put in Frontierland. The biggest difference is the ride vehicle, where two passengers can sit side by side, rather than in single file, allowing more capacity per vehicle. The attraction's soundtrack is also somewhat different in Orlando, with bluegrass-style country music featuring banjos and harmonicas used as a call back to both its Frontierland setting and Florida's proximity to Georgia, where the tales of Uncle Remus first gained popularity. The backing music heard in Disneyland's Splash Mountain owes more to the jazzy stylings of the nearby New Orleans Square.

DINOSAUR
April 22, 1998

Like The Indiana Jones Adventure in Disneyland, Animal Kingdom's dark attraction, DINOSAUR, is a combination track ride and motion simulator. Guests steer vehicles dubbed Time Rovers to journey back to the prehistoric past and find a living dinosaur before the species becomes extinct. The attraction ties in with the animated Disney feature of the same name, though it was opened prior to its theatrical release and initially titled Countdown to Extinction.

We begin our adventure in the Dino Institute, a research facility devoted to the study of these prehistoric creatures. In a pre-show video, a woman named Dr Marsh begins to describe the peaceful tour back through time we're about to take in our Time Rover, when another scientist named Dr. Seeker interrupts and tells us that we're now to journey back to a different period and rescue an Iguanodon, the same species as Aladar, the dinosaur from the Disney film. The two scientists argue over the safety of the proposed mission, and when Dr. Marsh leaves, Dr. Seeker informs us that he has hacked the time-travel mechanism and that we'll be carrying out his plan.

We board our Time Rovers and enter the time tunnel, where we see series of flashing lights, followed by a field of stars on the walls that presage our arrival in a prehistoric jungle.

Mist and heat set the scene as Dr. Seeker guides the Time Rover through the jungle in his search for the Iguanodon. Then comes the first encounter with a dinosaur, as a Styracosaurus pushes a falling tree dangerously close to the Time Rover. Another dinosaur searches beneath the ground for prey and a lone Velociraptor contemplates from a nearby ledge who in the vehicle might be his next meal.

Before long, Seeker locks in on a homing signal that he thinks will lead the guests to his prize. The Time Rover speeds forward, but instead of an Iguanodon we come face to face with a dangerous Carnotaurus. The ride vehicle eludes the massive predator and stops briefly near a plant-eating Saltosaurus, but Dr. Seeker urges us forward to accomplish our mission before an impending meteor strike.

A thunderstorm is heard as the Time Rover enters a clearing in the jungle and the vehicle changes course to just before a Cearadactylus swoops down from the sky. As we move forward, a group of tiny Compsognathus are startled by the sudden intruders and leap over our heads.

Another close encounter with the Carnotaurus follows and the Time Rover zigs and zags to evade his rage, while Dr. Seeker tries to abort the mission. The vehicle ventures down a path amid large trees toppling over, and finally we see the Iguanodon, struggling against the weight of a log so the Time Rover can pass beneath it as the meteor is about to hit. We brace ourselves as the meteor strikes and a flash of light reveals the Carnotaurus lunging as Dr. Seeker attempts to activate the time-travel sequence.

Then there is darkness and stars and the surrounding field of light alerts us that we are once again within the time tunnel. We see that the Iguanodon has made it back with us and is wandering the halls of the Dino Institute as the grateful Dr. Seeker goes off to find him.

Shortly after the release of the film in the spring of 2000, the attraction saw many changes. Some like the name change, new signage and statues of a Carnotaurus and an Iguanodon, were intended to better link the ride to the film, but others, such as a softening of the intensity of the pitch and verve of the vehicle, and the addition of a less frightening soundtrack, were made to accommodate the greater number of children who would now be interested in the ride.

Buzz Lightyear's Space Ranger Spin
November 3, 1998

The version of the ride found in Magic Kingdom's Tomorrowland was the first of the Buzz Lightyear dark rides to debut in any Disney theme park. The attraction's layout dates back to 1972, when it was originally the show building for If You Had Wings. After losing the sponsorship of Eastern Airlines, that aviation-themed ride was reconfigured as If You Could Fly, which remained in operation until Delta Airlines sponsored a new attraction named Delta Dream Flight, until it too gave up sponsorship. Two more name changes followed until the concept was abandoned in favor of the galaxy's favorite Space Ranger.

The Many Adventures of Winnie the Pooh
June 4, 1999

Owing largely to a newfound popularity thanks to a series of home video releases and cartoon programs, Winnie the Pooh's resurgent celebrity status called for plans to build an attraction in Walt Disney World's Magic Kingdom. While Orlando's Fantasyland was large enough to accommodate a new attraction, Disney executives instead decided to make the controversial move of closing Mr. Toad's Wild Ride. Though this move was met with no small amount of protest by fans of that classic dark ride, the first incarnation of a Winnie the Pooh-themed attraction opened in 1999.

Gran Fiesta Tour Starring the Three Caballeros
April 6, 2007

An update of Epcot's opening day attraction, El Rio del Tiempo, guests are enticed south of the border by a concert featuring Donald Duck and his friends Jose Carioca and Panchito Pistoles.

After boarding the boats that will take us on our journey, we are introduced to two of our new friends, only to discover that Donald has wandered off on his own. We see Donald enjoying himself on a whirlwind tour of Mexico, while Jose and Panchito search for him. After passing through a scene featuring dolls reminiscent of those found in "it's a small world," Donald proves an adventurous guide, introducing us to the country's ancient pyramids, and after some misadventures parasailing, cliff jumping, and scuba diving, all meant to showcase the natural wonders of the landscape, his friends finally catch up with him as he has stopped to try his luck with some local ladies enjoying the music of a live-action mariachi band.

As the journey concludes and the boat nears its destination in Mexico City, fireworks glow in the evening sky as the Three Caballeros finally perform their promised concert.

The Little Mermaid ~ Ariel's Undersea Adventure
December 6, 2012

Without the space restrictions that inhibit Disneyland, the Imagineers have always enjoyed more freedom world building in Orlando. The Magic Kingdom version of this colorful dark ride is housed within a re-creation of Prince Eric's castle. Ariel can be seen as a ship's figurehead, marking the entrance to the queue, which winds alongside waterfalls and caves beneath the castle. Guests on busy days, or those in no particular hurry, can help Scuttle and a group of crabs clean up Ariel's human stuff, which had been scattered about during a recent storm. Beyond this queue, the attraction is similar to its counterpart in Disneyland's California Adventure.

Frozen Ever After
June 21, 2016

In September 2014, Walt Disney World executives announced that Maelstrom, a popular but arguably outdated dark ride located in Epcot's Norway Pavilion would be closing, to be replaced by an attraction themed around the characters from *Frozen*. While this took many fans by surprise, as the setting of the film seemed more appropriate for Fantasyland, Disney was undeterred by protests and Frozen Ever After opened in the summer of 2016, combining scenes inspired by both the feature film and its follow-up short, *Frozen Fever*.

The new dark ride uses the same layout as Maelstrom and modified versions of its boats. Guests are welcomed to Arendelle as Queen Elsa has declared an Official Summer Snow Day Reception in the Ice Palace to commemorate Anna's heroic act of true love that saved her sister.

Passing through Wandering Oaken's Token Trading Post and Sauna, we board our boats to hear the familiar melody of "Do You Want to Build a Snowman?" and soon Olaf is seen greeting us with modified lyrics welcoming them to Elsa's celebration as Sven the reindeer looks on. Next, we come upon Pabbie the troll, sharing the story of Anna's unselfish sacrifice and the true love that saved her sister. The boat now begins its ascent, with Elsa's ice palace glowing in the distance.

Soon, we see Anna and Kristoff singing a reworded version of "For the First Time in Forever," as the interior of the ice palace is revealed and Queen Elsa sings "Let It Go" from a balcony overhead, her magical powers setting off effects of ice, light, and color all around. Suddenly, the boat is whisked backward with a chill of icy air and is sent outside the palace where we encounter Elsa's enchanted snowman and palace guard, Marshmallow, and several Snowgies. Marshmallow blows another icy blast of air toward the boat and it rushes forward, with the kingdom of Arendelle now in view and the night sky full of fireworks. Finally, we see Anna and Elsa hand in hand, with Olaf delighting in the thought of snow in summer, before the boat returns to the dock and the festivities end.

Na'vi River Journey
May 27, 2017

Inspired by the world of James Cameron's 2009 science fiction film *Avatar* and its forthcoming four sequels, Na'vi River Journey is a water ride in the tradition of Pirates of the Caribbean that opened in Disney's Animal Kingdom in the spring of 2017.

In the Valley of Mo'ara, we climb aboard reed boats and venture deep within the rainforests of Pandora, traveling along the sacred Kaspavan River. Along the way, we explore the natural wonders of this strange new world, passing through a series of caves and coming face to face with its wondrous wildlife including glowing plants and exotic rainforest inhabitants. We experience the culture of the Na'vi and commune with a shaman, who fills the surrounding forest with her song, demonstrating her deep connection to the force and spirit of Pandora.

Lost in Darkness
Walt Disney World's Shuttered Dark Rides

Though none of these attractions was without a devout follow-ing, many of Walt Disney World's dark rides have come and gone. Some were closed due to lack of popularity or to make way for newer and more exciting experiences, while others simply proved too costly to maintain. Still, as was the case with pioneering Disneyland attractions such as Adventure Thru Inner Space and Submarine Voyage Through Liquid Space, while all of these dark rides are gone, none are forgotten.

Mr. Toad's Wild Ride
October 1971 – September 7, 1998

Like its predecessor in Disneyland, Mr. Toad's Wild Ride was an opening day attraction in the Magic Kingdom, though it was not without its unique elements. Perhaps the most prom-inent was its two separate passenger boarding areas. This not only gave riders a different experience depending on which track they boarded from, but also added to the attraction's magnificent sense of chaos, as at one point on the ride, the cars running along the different tracks would be directly in each other's paths, giving those on board the fear of a collision. Mr. Toad's Wild Ride had all the selling points of a traditional dark ride. Arguably more cartoonish than other similar Disney attractions, instead of animatronics it made use of plywood characters and sets to bring the manic chaos through Toad Hall to life. Its two tracks allowed for rapid loading and main-tenance costs were low.

Still feeling the sting of public discontent after the closing of 20,000 Leagues Under the Sea, which was shuttered with no advance word or fanfare, upsetting many fans of that attraction, Disney brass decided to issue a media release to the *Orlando Sentinel* to inform park guests that it would be closing Mr Toad. Disney's intent was to replace the attraction with one featuring newer technology and centered around the increasingly popular and more family friendly world of Winnie the Pooh.

Disney believed that with advance notice, it would give fans of Mr. Toad the chance to enjoy one last ride. However, this approach backfired, as protests materialized almost immediately, from letter writing campaigns to "Toad-Ins" and the increasing attention of the media. As the protests grew, Disney instructed its security staff to pay extra attention to those who were known to be active protesters when they visited the park, independent of their frequent demonstrations. There were even some claims that Disney intentionally misled protesters into thinking that the attraction might not close after all, to help minimize the public relations issues.

Finally, with only a week's advance notice, Mr. Toad took his last ride on September 7, 1998. Its memory does live on, with paintings of Mr. Toad and Mole found within the Many Adventures of Winnie the Pooh, and a statue of Mr. Toad among those memorialized inside the Haunted Mansion's pet cemetery.

Snow White's Scary Adventures
October 1, 1971 – May 31, 2012

Another opening day dark ride at both Disneyland and Walt Disney World, the original version of Snow White's Scary Adventures in the Magic Kingdom differed considerably from its eventual re-imagining and was unquestionably much more frightening. In 1994, the attraction was dramatically redesigned to more closely mirror the Disneyland version, which was itself updated in 1983, but featured new scenes and others that were slightly out of sequence.

Like its Anaheim counterpart, the early incarnation of this dark ride put passengers in the position of Snow White, but Snow White's Scary Adventures was, like the Haunted Mansion, an example of how Disney's Imagineers looked at Disney World as more than just an opportunity to exploit the fact that they now had a larger castle and more space to let their ideas take shape. In addition to allowing them to craft entirely new guest experiences, they could revisit popular legacy attractions from the ground up. Comparisons between this incarnation of Snow White's Scary Adventures and Disney's quintessential dark ride, the Haunted Mansion, are valid in a number of ways, but as passengers aboard the mine carts were quite literally stalked by the malevolent Queen in her near ceaseless assault, and the ride ended in their "death," certainly none of the Haunted Mansion's Grim Grinning Ghosts can be said to present that degree of direct threat to their guests.

One marked difference between the Disneyland and initial Walt Disney World version of this attraction was that the sequence of events experienced was essentially reversed. The climax of the Anaheim version sees riders leaving the safety of the mine where they see a warning from Dopey about the evil Queen; in Orlando the mine was perhaps the most frightening scene, with the hag appearing three times, and attempting to drop a giant gemstone on passengers at the conclusion of the ride.

Even the exterior of the Orlando attraction served to lure unsuspecting guests into an environment they may have thought far more festive. Its elaborate presentation was among the most ornate in Fantasyland, heralding an experience fit for Walt Disney's original princess—but would instead lead to one more akin to the Haunted Mansion.

The attraction closed in May 2012 and was replaced by Princess Fairytale Hall as part of the Magic Kingdom's major Fantasyland expansion. Two years later, the opening of Seven Dwarfs Mine Train saw many of the dwarf and animal figures from the dark ride's "Silly Song" sequence repurposed for the new attraction.

20,000 Leagues Under the Sea: The Submarine Voyage

October 14, 1971 – September 5, 1994

Even as Walt Disney's Florida Project was barely under-way, Imagineers were working on an attraction to mirror Disneyland's then popular Submarine Voyage. One of the largest and most costly Disney attractions ever designed, the Orlando version featured 14 submarines (including two that tangled with sea monsters as part of the attraction's world building), 20,000 Leagues Under the Sea was ultimately most valuable not as an attraction, but as a cornerstone of Fantasyland's early iconography.

Unlike the nuclear-age-themed submarines transporting guests through the uncharted waters of Disneyland, those traveling through the Magic Kingdom would be boarding replicas of Captain Nemo's *Nautilus*, which not only provided Imagineers with more opportunities for theming within the attraction's Fantasyland environment, but gave Disney an opportunity to remind visitors of its classic 1954 film.

During construction, beaches were "built" along the shores of the picturesque lagoon, and abandoned pirate treasure and the words "20,000 Leagues" tempted guests passing by the site.

Opening two weeks after the Magic Kingdom due to issues with the lagoon's ability to hold water, and covering nearly a quarter of Fantasyland, the attraction was extremely popular with guests, who watched as cast members dressed as Nemo's crew operated the attraction.

In the queue area, seafaring tunes such as "Whale of a Tale" played as Captain Nemo shared his thoughts on the majestic nature of the sea and the adventures ahead. As guests navigated the queue area and took in a panoramic view of the lagoon area, amid the noise and the clamor they might begin to smell the fuel powering the submarines. After reaching the loading area, guests descended into the submarine and heard the sound of Captain Nemo's pipe organ echoing through the cabin, before the helmsman began issuing commands over a microphone.

Guests proceeded through the length of the craft and took a seat, facing their own porthole, where they would see the lingering activity of the surface just prior to their descent as the helmsman issued the standard Disney dark ride directives, and the sub hummed and readied for its voyage.

Captain Nemo gave directions to "secure ship for sea" and the submarine launched into the lagoon, heading downward as guests watched a flurry of bubbles in their portholes. Captain Nemo introduced himself and informed passengers as to the purpose of their voyage as the range and size of marine life visible through the porthole began to vary considerably.

After encountering curious moray eels in a reef, Nemo made the startling claim that fish actually talk, and then a recording was played for guests of what might have been a conversation among marine life, before encountering some of his crew divers tending to beds of seaweed in an aquatic garden.

Word of storms on the surface forced the submarine to dive still deeper just as a shark was caught within the tentacles of an octopus. More sharks were seen circling through a grave-yard of lost ships.

By now, those who had had experienced both this attraction and its less whimsical predecessor in Anaheim would have observed similarities, despite Orlando's more blatant ties to the Jules Verne novel and Disney film. Where Disneyland's Tomorrowland version cast its divers as treasure hunters, here they were farmers. And while there were only minimal advances in Imagineering technology in the years between the development of the two attractions, the increased size of the Florida show building alone created depth-of-field that height-ened the illusion in there, thanks to forced perspective.

Nemo remarked on the visual marvel of the Aurora Borealis, which lit the scene of a Viking ship the submarine passed in the graveyard, but it's a wonder that guests would not experi-ence for long as the threat of icebergs against the hull of the submarine was too risky and the captain ordered yet another dive, this time into the black depths of the sea. Now, glowing jellyfish and other eerie creatures would pass through the view of the portholes as Nemo and his crew navigated this realm of eternal darkness. The descent could only be sustained so long, and as the submarine ascended, passengers found themselves amid the remains of a forgotten ancient civilization with broken statues and mighty figures of myth and legend littering the ocean floor, which Nemo suggested was the lost continent of Atlantis. Then he cautioned that Atlantis may be merely the stuff of fantasy, much like sea serpents and mermaids, just as a whirling green tail was seen by passengers through the portholes, with its decidedly less-than-ferocious upper half positioned squarely between two mermaids.

A crew member warned Captain Nemo of unusual tur-bulence, which passengers discover to be the same volcano that sent Atlantis to its watery grave. Pillars in the distance trembled and swayed due to the renewed volcanic activity threatening the safe passage of the *Nautilus*. Nemo ordered his crew to a red alert.

While this crisis was averted, word was then received that another of Nemo's submersibles had been attacked by a giant squid. Yet another squid began an assault on the *Nautilus* itself, and Nemo ordered a "full repellent charge" in a desperate attempt to free his craft from the enormous red tentacles now engulfing it. The submarine rose to the surface in a storm of bubbles.

An extraordinarily complex attraction to maintain due to its mix of massive ride vehicles, underwater environments, and animation, a good deal of time and effort were required to keep it up to the standards of a Disney theme park. It was subject to regular downtimes to allow for renovations and due to its size these were always among the most visible in the park.

Disney eventually considered the attraction too expensive to operate, as its effects were becoming dated and its maintenance was labor-intensive. The replicas of the Harper Goff-designed *Nautilus* were put in storage, and others were sold off at auction or discarded; two would see use eventually in the Studio Backlot Tour at Hollywood Studios and as scenery at Disney's Castaway Cay.

A spouting statue of King Triton was soon installed in the lagoon area, which was newly rechristened Ariel's Grotto, and another section became a meet-and-greet space for characters from the nearby Winnie the Pooh attraction.

In 2004, a decade after the attraction's closing, the lagoon was drained and Disney issued commemorative pins as the show building was demolished and the lagoon was filled in to be readied for expansion. A year later brought the temporary children's play area known as Pooh's Playful Spot, which included a tribute to its predecessor in the form of a *Nautilus*-shaped knot in a tree, before it too was razed to make way for the Seven Dwarfs Mine Train.

Currently, a mural found in the loading area of the nearby Under the Sea ~ Journey of the Little Mermaid features still another tribute to this ambitious Walt Disney World original.

If You Had Wings

June 5, 1972 – June 1, 1987

Located in Tomorrowland, If You Had Wings was the first new attraction to open in the Magic Kingdom that was not the result of a delay following its grand opening. Corporate sponsorships had contributed a great deal to the success of Disney theme parks since the ABC television network loaned Walt Disney the money that made the construction of Disneyland possible. Over the years, the number and variety of those sponsorships grew as they were seen to be beneficial to all involved, whether it was Disneyland's Enchanted Tiki Room, first sponsored by United Airlines and then later and more deliciously by Dole Food Company, or Disney's partners in the 1964-1965 New York World's Fair, which led to "it's a small world" (Pepsi-Cola), Carousel of Progress (General Electric), and Ford Magic Skyway (Ford Motor Company), portions of which were used in Primeval World. Its latest partner, Eastern Airlines, was eager to promote its travel destinations to exotic locales, and Disney World's planners were just as anxious to fill vacant space in Tomorrowland with something new and exciting for park guests, who would board the still fairly new omnimover ride vehicles to travel to Eastern Air Lines' destinations around the world.

Another of the attractions designed by legendary Imagineer and dark ride innovator Claude Coats, who had also been instrumental in Disney World's re-imagining of Snow White's Scary Adventures, the attraction began with a pre-show acquainting guests with Eastern Air Lines before a gentle takeoff over seagulls and other planes seen in silhouette.

Passengers would travel through filmed and animated scenes of New Orleans, Mexico, Bermuda, Jamaica, Puerto Rico, Trinidad, and the Bahamas, before entering the Speed Room, where they experienced a first-person perspective of various modes of transportation in a way that was almost like a crude form of virtual reality, and finally the Mirror Room, which created a sensation of being lifted over scenes of mountains and deserts, before their journey came to an end and they were told to disembark. Designed to appeal to potential tourists, riders stepped off their vehicles into an area with an Eastern Air Lines reservation desk, complete with agents ready to assist with their travel plans.

In the summer of 1987, Eastern Airlines ended its sponsorship due to financial problems, which necessitated the attraction's refurbishment and rechristening as If You Could Fly, with all of the references to the ride's original sponsor removed. The Eastern Airlines logo was replaced by an image of a seagull.

This incarnation of the attraction remained operational until January 1989, when it too was shuttered to make way for a further revamp, known as Dreamflight and sponsored by Delta Airlines, which would open in June of that year.

Guests would enter Delta Dreamflight as if they were walking into an airport terminal. After they walked through the queue, glancing at Delta's many exciting global destinations, they would board their ride vehicle for a tour through what can best be described as a stylized pop-up book detailing the history of flight, beginning with hot air balloons and other curious contraptions, before progressing to the earliest biplanes and barnstormers. Stunt planes came next, then passenger airlines.

From the rooftops of Paris, passengers were given notice to "prepare for supersonic takeoff" on their Dreamflight into the future, with projections of fireworks exploding all around them and images of a futuristic city revealing Delta's seemingly limitless potential as they reached the final portion of the attraction and yet another pop-up book, with a Delta jet seen flying off into the clouds.

Dreamflight remained in operation until June of 1996; months after Delta had abandoned sponsorship of the attraction. Minor cosmetic changes followed and its name was changed to Take Flight, until its closing in January 1998 to make way for Buzz Lightyear's Space Ranger Spin.

El Rio Del Tiempo

October 1, 1982 – January 2, 2007

An opening day attraction, El Rio Del Tiempo, or the River of Time, was a slow-moving boat ride in Epcot's Mexico Pavilion that took passengers on a journey through some of Mexico's history. Guests boarded boats and passed a pyramid deep in a Yucatan jungle with a smoking volcano in the background. Traveling through various dioramas depicting scenes of Mexican life and culture, the attraction mixed the audio-animatronics of "it's a small world" with projection screens to engage with passengers before the finale in Mexico City, where marionettes danced against a backdrop of fireworks in the nighttime sky.

The attraction closed in early 2007 to be re-imagined as Gran Fiesta Tour Starring the Three Caballeros, with only minimal tweaking. The marionettes seen during the finale were removed and the projections seen throughout were changed.

World of Motion

October 1, 1982 – January 2, 1996

The only realized attraction that Disney animator Ward Kimball ever worked on, World of Motion was a General Motors-sponsored dark ride conceived as a humorous look at the history of transportation. Guests boarded their omni-mover (here dubbed chaircars) as the attraction's theme song "It's Fun to Be Free" played and the vehicle made a quick u-turn taking them outside of the building before bringing them back inside and entering a cave to the first scene of transportation, foot power, as cavemen tried to cool down their feet. This was followed by attempts to travel over water and scenes of people trying to control such animals as camels and zebras.

Time marched on and passengers saw the invention of the wheel: after it was put up against a triangle and a square, the wheel was the clear winner when it came to forward momentum.

Following that, guests saw humankind take to the sea, to face not only the treachery of unknown shores, but mysterious sea serpents. Later on, even the potential for flight was not enough to excite Mona Lisa, whom Leonardo da Vinci unwisely managed to ignore while engrossed in his scientific endeavors. From there, progress shifted to steam power on the Mississippi River and eventually a steam locomotive.

Kimball's humor was present throughout the attraction, especially in scenes like the depiction of the world's first traffic jam, which was set in roughly 1910. Here, children screamed amid a neighing horse, spilled ice truck, and general calamity, before the chaircars moved on through more familiar scenes of the mid-20th century before entering speed tunnels similar to those used in If You Had Wings. Inside the tunnels, the chaircars careened down a snowmobile trail and rafted down a river, before ending their journey at CenterCore, a glowing city of the future. The end of the ride featured a mirror effect similar to the hitchhiking ghosts for the Haunted Mansion. Guests disembarked into TransCenter, an exhibition hall that showcased then-current developments in transportation.

Much as it was for its aviation industry partners, business for General Motors had been sluggish enough to reframe their sponsorship as a series of one-year contracts, until the decision was made in 1996 to shut down World of Motion completely and create a new attraction that focused solely on cars. General Motors continued its sponsorship of the popular new attraction Test Track until its refurbishment in 2012. Chevrolet now sponsors Test Track. Some references to World of Motion remain on murals within the ride and elsewhere; in addition, some of the audio-animatronic characters and other elements from the attraction have been recycled in Disney theme parks around the world.

Horizons
October 1, 1983 – January 9, 1999

With the opening of Tomorrowland in 1955, Walt Disney envisioned the look and feel of the Space Age for generations to come, but as reality too quickly synced with Disneyland's extraordinary vision of the future, Tomorrowland was gradually re-imagined as less an idealized city of the future to more a realm of science fiction and fantasy. Even as Tomorrowland evolved, it would not be the end of Walt's vision of the future. Epcot, or the Experimental Prototype Community of Tomorrow, was originally planned as a utopian city built using new and innovative technologies and transportation systems, to serve as a showcase of urban design and organization. After Walt's death, though the plans for Epcot evolved into its current status as that of a permanent World's Fair, the interest in exploring humanity's march toward the future did not wane and would manifest in no small degree through Horizons.

Known during its earliest conceptual phases as Century 3 and Future Probe, Horizons was a sequel of sorts to the Carousel of Progress and opened on the first anniversary of Epcot. This omnimover dark ride gave guests a bright and uplifting glimpse into what the future of what Earth might be like based on scientific advancements. Much like Walt Disney's original vision of Epcot, it depicted a vision of humanity moving beyond our historically divisive lines of class, race, and cultural differences toward truly sustainable communities on Earth and beyond.

Departing from the Future Port for the 21st century, the overhead omnimover vehicles made their way through scenes showcasing different visions of the future from years past, beginning in the era of Jules Verne with a callback to his classic novel (and later namesake to one of the most successful dark rides of all time) *A Trip To The Moon*. Voices reminiscent of the father and mother from Carousel of Progress, though now slightly older, were heard as the narrators, escorting guests on this journey as they witnessed humanity's early attempts at flight, took a look at the "far-out" future as perceived in the 1950s, and culminated in the launch of a space shuttle. Guests were then treated to glimpses of the promises of the future seen on two giant IMAX screens, ranging from unlocking the secrets of DNA to the power of microprocessors and computer technologies.

Attention turned to the space station Brava Centauri and the space community of Nova Cite, with a look inside the narrator's living room before the journey continued to the desert farming environment of Mesa Verde. From there, the scene shifted to Sea Castle, a floating city, where the mysteries of the ocean were explored. Finally, guests saw the vastness of distant galaxies, as the omnimover explored space colonies of the future and saw how the materials mined from outer space might be used back on Earth.

Horizons was the only Disney attraction of its time with multiple endings, allowing passengers to select which path they wanted to take back to the Future Port. At the push of a button, they could select a video that treated them to a speeding flyover sequence of Brava Centauri, Mesa Verde, or Sea Castle. Whichever option got the most votes in the ride vehicle was the winner.

Horizons was also the only Future World attraction to explore all of the pavilion's elements, along with humanity's relationship to land, air, ocean, and space. Like Carousel of Progress, it was initially sponsored by General Electric, and passengers could hear the theme song "There's a Great Big Beautiful Tomorrow" from the legacy attraction playing on a television set during the 1950s sequence. General Electric ceased its sponsorship in September 1993 and Horizons closed in December 1994, with no official explanation, although the lack of a corporate sponsor is widely believed to have been the reason.

It would reopen a year later while both Universe of Energy and World of Motion were being refurbished. The sun set for the final time on Horizons on January 9, 1999, due to reported structural problems and a sinkhole beneath the building, though it would eventually make way for Mission: SPACE in the summer of 2003.

Maelstrom
July 5, 1988 – October 5, 2014

A trip through Norway's history, from its roots in ancient mythology to celebrated tales of Vikings and the modern era, Maelstrom mixed an audio-animatronic enhanced log flume ride with promotional film, and was another attempt by Disney to make a dark ride that was both educational and entertaining.

Passengers on this World Showcase attraction boarded boats patterned after Viking ships and began their journey by traveling up an incline to witness the life of the Norwegian seafarer and maritime villages from Norway's distant past.

The boats next passed through dangerous, magical troll country, but before they could escape, a three-headed troll cast a spell and made them disappear, or more accurately sent them hurtling backward, past scenes of living trees, penguins, and polar bears, before rotating back to a forward-facing position and taking a twenty-eight-foot plunge into the stormy North Sea and passing an oil rig to represent entry into the modern world, before the boat settled in the calm waters of a sleepy Norwegian village. After guests exited their boats, they had the option of watching a five-minute film, *The Spirit of Norway*, which highlighted various aspects of Norwegian tourism.

For reasons ranging from the age of its accompanying film to the inescapable popularity of the subject matter of its replacement attraction, Maelstrom closed permanently on October 5, 2014, to make room for Frozen Ever After, which opened on June 21, 2016.

Ellen's Energy Adventure
September 15, 1996 – August 13, 2017

This sole attraction in Epcot's Universe of Energy Pavilion evolved from what was initially a more serious look at human-kind's relationship with the various forms of energy. From Epcot's opening day through 1996, guests who visited the original attraction could watch films and ride through a diorama featuring audio-animatronic dinosaurs.

Then, in the fall of 1996, Disney opted for a lighter approach, rebranding the attraction as Ellen's Energy Adventure and recruiting Ellen DeGeneres, Bill Nye, and Jamie Lee Curtis to look at the history of energy production, fossil fuels, and renewable resources. In the attraction's pre-show video, Ellen fell asleep and dreamed that she was a contestant on an energy-themed version of the television game show *Jeopardy*, facing off against an old rival (Jamie Lee Curtis) and Albert Einstein. Ellen performed miserably against her rival, who happened to be a professor of energy at Princeton University, and so Bill Nye the Science Guy shows up to assist her. In the theater portion of the attraction, Nye explained the Big Bang and the origin of fossil fuels, and then guests moved through an updated diorama sequence featuring dinosaurs, before watching another film on sources of energy, and a final film where Ellen uses the knowledge she gained to win at *Jeopardy*.

Ellen's lengthy energy adventure, which had become dated and more popular as an escape from the hot Orlando sun than as a learning experience, closed to make way for an attraction themed around *Guardians of the Galaxy*, the first Marvel attraction to open in one of Disney's Orlando parks.

The Great Movie Ride
May 1, 1989 – August 13, 2017

With its façade serving as an homage to Hollywood's landmark Chinese Theater, guests visiting this Hollywood Studios' dark ride boarded vehicles for a whirlwind tour through re-imagined sets of classic movies like *The Wizard of Oz, Casablanca, Tarzan, Alien,* and *Raiders of the Lost Ark*. Animatronic figures of stars as diverse as John Wayne, Gene Kelly, and Julie Andrews helped set the stage for this journey through the golden age of cinema.

Over the years, movie-buffs delighted in seeing props from many memorable films, including Dorothy's ruby slippers, Sam's piano from *Casablanca*, Iceman's uniform from *Top Gun*, Indiana Jones' machete, monkey heads from *Indiana Jones and the Temple of Doom*, and Mary Poppins' horse from the carousel ride sequence of the classic Disney film.

From 2001 to 2015, the façade of the Chinese Theater was blocked by an enormous replica of the Sorcerer's Hat, which had long served as the park's symbol.The hat was demolished after an agreement with Turner Classic Movies, which also included updates to the attraction's pre-show video and ride finale.

As guests approached the end of the queue, they found themselves inside a replica of a 1930s era Hollywood soundstage and boarded ride vehicles modeled after theater seats, with a guide seated up front to narrate the tour and control the vehicle. The tour began with a look at famous musicals. Audio-animatronic chorus girls performed a routine from *Footlight Parade*; Gene Kelly clung to a lamp post in a scene from *Singin' in the Rain*; and Julie Andrews and Dick Van Dyke cavorted on the rooftops of London, singing "Chim Chim Cher-ee" from *Mary Poppins*.

Next, passengers visited a seedy back alley that served as the setting for a tribute to gangster films and watched a scene from *The Public Enemy*, punctuated by an audio-animatronic

James Cagney. Just up ahead, as the tour guide stopped for a red light, a Disney cast member playing a gangster and her audio-animatronic sidekicks got involved in a shootout with a rival gang. The cast member car-jacks the ride vehicle to facilitate their escape and the tour continued through a setting in the Wild West, where passengers encounted audio-animatronic re-creations of Clint Eastwood and John Wayne.

From the Old West, the ride made its way to the distant reaches of outer space where passengers found themselves on board the *Nostromo*, the spaceship from the movie *Alien*. The gangster who hijacked the ride vehicle doesn't like the sound of this and speeds through the ship's corridors, but not before the resident alien appears and attacks the passengers. As they exit the ship, observant riders saw Sigourney Weaver's Ripley character wielding a flamethrower as she prepared to confront the alien invader.

Moving onward, the ride transitioned to an ancient temple filled with snakes, and guests enjoyed a scene from *Raiders of the Lost Ark*, where Indiana Jones and Sallah discover the Ark of the Covenant. As they moved through the temple ruins, a shimmering jewel attracts the attention of the gangster who hijacked the vehicle. The gangster is warned by a figure guarding the jewel that those who disturb its sanctity will pay with their lives. Ignoring that, the gangster reaches for the jewel and is engulfed by a cloud of smoke, leaving only skeletal remains. The temple guard is revealed to be the original tour guide and the ride continued through a horror film set and the jungle world of Tarzan, where Jane and Cheeta could be seen before Tarzan himself heroically swings by on a vine.

Passengers then witnessed the final scene from *Casablanca* as audio-animatronic figures of Humphrey Bogart and Ingrid Bergman stood in front of an airplane readying for takeoff. Guests were treated to a brief glimpse of Mickey Mouse in his first feature film role as the Sorcerer's Apprentice from *Fantasia*, before moving on to the Land of Oz.

In Oz, riders first found themselves in Munchkinland, as Dorothy's house has just landed on the Wicked Witch of the East and the Munchkins rejoiced at their good fortune, only to have their celebration spoiled by a cloud of smoke that heralds the arrival of the Wicked Witch of the West, who demanded to know who killed her sister as the citizens of Munchkinland cower in fear. The tour guide answered her and she disappeared angrily, again shrouded in a cloud of smoke. The tour continued along the Yellow Brick Road where riders saw audio-animatronic figures of Dorothy, Toto, Scarecrow, Tin Woodsman, and the Cowardly Lion, with Emerald City in sight at last.

The grand finale saw both sets of ride vehicles enter a large theater, lining up side-by-side to watch a montage of classic film moments, many of which were represented during the ride experience. The ride ended back on the same soundstage that it began.

This attraction served as the original inspiration for Disney MGM (later Hollywood) Studios. Initial plans had called for a show business-themed pavilion in Epcot, but Disney executives thought the idea was good enough to fashion an entirely new park around. Financial difficulties would lead to the abandonment of plans for this attraction to make its way to Disneyland Paris, but even after those early financial hurdles were overcome and the theatrically themed Walt Disney Studios opened in France, this attraction was not built. Budget cuts dating back to the 1980s also doomed repeated attempts to bring it to California.

Back in Orlando, a 3D update called the Chinese Theater's Villain Ride was planned as a replacement for the Great Movie Ride, but it was also never built. The addition of Turner Classic Movies as a sponsor in 2015 brought with it a number of alterations, though little of the ride itself was impacted as the changes focused primarily on the queue area, pre-show, and the film clips used in the finale.

Despite its recent rebranding and partnership with Turner Classic Movies, it was announced in the summer of 2017 that the curtain would fall forever on the Great Movie Ride to make way for a new dark ride, Mickey and Minnie's Runaway Railway.

CHAPTER SIX

Dark Rides in the Land of the Rising Sun

Located just outside Tokyo, in Urayasu, Chiba, Japan, Tokyo Disneyland opened on April 15, 1983. A second park, Tokyo DisneySea, opened September 4, 2001. While Tokyo Disneyland borrows its design heavily from its American predecessors, featuring similar lands and attractions and the hub-and-spoke design used in both Disneyland and Walt Disney World, with a World Bazaar taking the place of Main Street, U.S.A., Tokyo DisneySea employs a theme of nautical exploration, which is evident in each of that park's dark rides.

Tokyo Disneyland's Dark Rides

The Haunted Mansion
April 15, 1983

This opening day attraction in the Fantasyland section of Tokyo Disneyland is very similar to the Orlando version of the dark ride, although it is not without some significant differences. Immediately of note is that while great care is taken of the landscaping of other incarnations of the Haunted Mansions, the grounds of Tokyo are overgrown with weeds and the mansion itself shows signs of decay with broken windows and desecrated crypts. Unlike other mansions, there is also no trace of Master Gracey, rumored one-time human inhabitant of the now ghostly retreat.

Two stone gargoyles stand on the pillars of the gate, periodically turning their heads to look on guests as they pass through to experience Tokyo's take on this perennially popular ride.

"it's a small world"
April 15, 1983

A near replica of the Orlando attraction, Tokyo Disneyland brings "it's a small world" to life with only a few differences. Most significantly, its exterior is based on the classic design of the Disneyland original, and the ride's finale, presented in a much smaller Goodbye Room, is sung in Japanese.

Peter Pan's Flight
April 15, 1983

Nearly identical to the Walt Disney World version, this attraction was renovated in early 2016 to feature new digital effects throughout the ride and a new nighttime Neverland scene.

Pinocchio's Daring Journey
April 15, 1983

Though plans for this dark ride had begun as far back as 1976, it was put in storage until the 1983 refurbishment of Anaheim's Fantasyland. The Tokyo Disneyland version opened a little more than a month earlier. Save for its different façade, a few minor cosmetic differences, and the Japanese dialogue, the attraction is essentially the same as California's.

Pirates of the Caribbean
April 15, 1983

A near replica of the Anaheim original, from the ornate Louisiana townhouse that serves as the attraction's exterior, to the clinking silverware heard in the Blue Bayou restaurant as the passenger boats launch from their swampy berth, though it lacks a second drop. Of note is that this ride is currently sponsored by Kirin Beverage, showing that the American parks are not alone in their habit of seeking corporate partnerships.

Snow White's Adventures
April 15, 1983

Tokyo Disneyland's version of the classic Snow White dark ride represents something of a missing link of those attractions that came before it. It is not quite the taste of gothic horror imagined by Claude Coats for Walt Disney World in 1971, nor is it as close a chronological adaptation of the events of the film as the 1983 update of the ride would be. Instead, it's a mix of both versions.

The ride begins in the queen's castle, with her peering down through her curtain as the vehicles enter and we turn the corner to witness her transformation into the vain old hag. Then we move on to the dungeon, where she hatches her plot against Snow White and prepares the deadly apple.

The scene transitions to the frightening forest with its demonic trees, ominous howling, and eerie music, before we enter the dwarfs' cottage to see Snow White watching from the stairs as they dance the night away. This peaceful scene is all too brief. We see the villainous hag, heralded by her menacing cackle, lurking outside the cottage.

As we make our way to the mines and marvel at the assortment of sparkling gems, the hag once again tempts us with the poisoned apple before we are seemingly crushed by the giant boulder as she stands high on the cliff above.

Splash Mountain
October 1, 1992

Tokyo Disneyland's incarnation of Splash Mountain found in Critter Country is almost a mirror image of Disney World's Splash, with a few exceptions. While the barn-like structure so reminiscent of classic mill chute rides is used as the main entrance, unlike Orlando's version, it is absent for the ride's second ascent. Instead, the passenger logs float through a cave-like opening.

Ride dialogue and lyrics to "How Do You Do" and "Zip a Dee Doo Dah" are in Japanese, but English for "Everybody's Got a Laughin' Place." The music and vocals are matched with different scenes and slightly different arrangements are used.

And though they are in their familiar bayou setting, the secondary critter characters are arranged differently and the scenes presented in a distinctly new order.

Roger Rabbit's Car Toon Spin
April 15, 1996

Identical to the Anaheim version, this attraction is located in Tokyo Disneyland's Toontown.

Pooh's Hunny Hunt
September 4, 2000

A more elaborate version of the Many Adventures of Winnie the Pooh attraction than those in the American parks, Tokyo Disneyland's dark ride visit to the Hundred Acre Wood uses enhanced audio-animatronic figures and a trackless ride system.

After walking through the queue area, which is made to resemble a storybook detailing the adventures of Pooh and his friends, we board hunny pot vehicles and pass through the pages of an open book to find ourselves in the Hundred Acre Wood, in the middle of the blustery day. Holding tightly to a balloon given to him by Christopher Robin, Pooh floats overhead. As he is whisked away by the wind, Rabbit, Piglet, and Owl seem to have their own problems, and Tigger bounces into view, leaving a horde of bees in his wake.

The scene shifts to a more ominous setting, with Pooh fast asleep in a darkened room. Suddenly, a field of stars appears and Pooh is raised into the air and slowly begins to spin before disappearing. As this occurs, eyes, a mouth, and an elephant's trunk appear on his balloon.

Of course, this is all a prelude to Pooh's dream of Heffalumps and Woozles, and this portion of the attraction features not only the traditional audio-animatronic characters, but animated projections as Pooh watches from above in something of a fugue state.

Our hunny pots are roused quickly from their "slumber" and sent backwards through a tunnel, where projections of Pooh and the creatures from the dream sequence pass overhead, and we see Pooh once more in his element, happily enjoying honey inside the honey tree. The final scene returns to the opening picture-book theme, telling us we have reached the end of the story, with all of our friends from the Hundred Acre Wood bidding us farewell.

Buzz Lightyear's Astro Blasters
April 15, 2004

Found in Tomorrowland, and one of the most popular attractions at Tokyo Disneyland, this dark ride is a copy of the Anaheim version, save for its Japanese language track.

Monsters, Inc. Ride & Go Seek!
April 15, 2009

Returning us to the world of Monstropolis sometime after the events of *Monsters, Inc.*, this dark ride in Tokyo Disneyland's Tomorrowland invites guests to play an interactive game of flashlight tag as we explore the city with Boo, Mike, Sully, and other characters from the Disney/Pixar film. Somewhat reminiscent of the Buzz Lightyear attractions, this ride emphasizes the interactivity and storytelling elements, immersing passengers in the game of hide and seek being played by Mike, Sully, and Boo, and allowing them to participate, but does not include the opportunity to accumulate points.

Of course it is not every day that humans are in Monstropolis, so as we enter the factory, an instructional video on flashlight tag featuring Mike Wazowski is shown. Once we understand the premise, we make our way to the ride vehicles, each of which is equipped with two flashlights.

The ride experience begins in the Scare Factory where Mike and Sully work. As we enter the Simulator Room, it seems that Boo would rather go explore the factory than join in on the game, and she giggles as Sully warns her not to wander off too far. Rounding a corner, we see that Mike and Sully's rival and coworker, Randall, has returned and is intent on capturing Boo to extract her screams. His evil laughter can be heard echoing throughout the factory.

As Mike pulls the lever of a power generator, the city outside goes dark. The ride continues through the men's locker room and lockers open and close, revealing monsters. Sully searches the room for Boo with a flashlight of his own and we can hear her giggling, while Randall hides beneath a pile of towels. On the laugh floor, Sully continues his search for Boo underneath tables and Mike has his fingers caught in a door as Smitty tries to help him, while Needleman fiddles with a control panel. We pass Randall again, now carrying a butterfly net as the action transitions to the biggest scene on the streets of the city.

Like the Anaheim attraction, we see a re-creation of Harryhausen's restaurant, where the sushi chef looks for Boo beneath food containers. Nearby, Sully emerges from beneath a sewer and Mike is seen with his girlfriend Celia, whom guests can dunk in water by using their flashlights, before he foils another attempt by Randall to capture Boo, knocking him into a trash compactor.

As we turn away from the trash compactor and a defeated Randall, we see Mike, Sully, and Boo wishing each other goodbye at her door, before another turn takes us past Boo and a smaller monster, who wave goodbye. We then meet the interactive Roz audio-animatronic familiar to guests of the Anaheim attraction, and exit the ride.

Tokyo DisneySea's Dark Rides

Journey to the Center of the Earth
September 4, 2001

The stories of Jules Verne had an indelible impact on Walt Disney, manifesting as they did not only in his on-screen adaptation of *20,000 Leagues Under the Sea*, but later in both Disneyland and Walt Disney World. That passion for one of the world's best-known authors of tales of science fiction and fantasy would later translate to another attraction at Tokyo DisneySea, based on Verne's *Journey to the Center of the Earth*.

Once planned as a free-fall attraction as part of the abandoned Discovery Mountain project at Disneyland Paris, this tribute to Jules Verne would later resurface with a different ride technology. And as much as it owes its inspiration to Verne, the ride also has an impressive pedigree in its score, composed by Buddy Baker, who was responsible for the music of the Haunted Mansion and If You Had Wings.

We wind our way deep within the caverns of volcanic Mount Prometheus on Mysterious Island, which serves as Captain Nemo's base. After walking through labs with his curious research in view, we board terravators, or elevators, to the base station where there are warnings of increased volcanic activity. We then climb aboard steam-powered mining vehicles to traverse the tunnels carved deep within the heart of the earth.

We begin in the Crystal Caverns surrounded by glowing crystal formations, then enter a subterranean forest of giant, colorful mushrooms inhabited by strange creatures. Suddenly, an earthquake strikes, causing a cave-in of the path ahead. A detour takes us through a new route filled with giant egg sacs, as the near miss of a lightning strike on the shores of an underground lake propels the mining vehicle into the heart of the volcano and almost into the waiting grasp of an enormous lava monster that roars and reaches for us menacingly before our vehicle bursts forward one last time on the wave of a volcanic eruption and returns us safely to the surface, where we see a brief glimpse of daylight before returning to the attraction's docking bay and exiting the vehicle.

Indiana Jones Adventure: Temple of the Crystal Skull
September 4, 2001

Indiana Jones' assistant, Paco, is in business giving tours of the Lost Temple of the Crystal Skull—which, legend has it, is home to the Fountain of Youth—inside the ruins of an imposing Aztec temple in the Lost River Delta port-of-call. While the name of the attraction is similar to the fourth movie in the Indiana Jones series of films, the ride opened several years prior to its release and its story bears no resemblance.

We board the same style of enhanced motion vehicle used in the Anaheim version of the attraction and embark on our journey into the Temple of the Crystal Skull, starting with the Chamber of Destiny and proceeding through a door with the stars of the night sky shining down overhead.

At the end of a hallway is the inescapable sight of the Crystal Skull, which at first seems to glow a demonic red before beaming bright rays of light. As it does so, the ride vehicle takes a sharp turn toward a large corridor. Crackles of lightning illuminate the walls and reveal giant busts of snakes overhead as a green mist fills the room.

Indiana Jones appears, scolding us for looking into the eyes of the Crystal Skull as he tries desperately to keep a pair of heavy doors behind him closed, and we accelerate forward up a flight of stairs. Decaying skeletons are seen, some of which pop out at passengers, and as we move forward through near total darkness, insects fill the room before we feel the sensation of puffs of air, as poisoned darts fly around us.

Emerging from the darkness, we find ourselves facing a chasm with a rope bridge separating us from the other side. The bridge sways beneath the weight of the vehicle, but we make it safely across, only to encounter a threatening snake with glowing red eyes that hisses as we pass and strikes at the vehicle.

Another turn, and we pass hundreds of human skulls adorning the walls of the temple. We drive beneath the rope bridge to see a face on the wall issue a threat before unleashing a fireball in our direction. We accelerate through the smoke into a corridor lined with glowing skulls, somehow activating a booby trap, and dodge more darts as we see Indiana Jones hanging from a vine above, cautioning us just before a massive boulder comes hurtling toward the vehicle and we plunge to safety.

After one last meeting with Dr. Jones, who stands beside the crushed boulder, we disembark and have the opportunity to purchase a photograph taken during the adventure.

Sinbad's Storybook Voyage
September 4, 2001

This attraction in Tokyo DisneySea's Arabian Coast was dramatically retooled from its much darker original incarnation, known as Sinbad's Seven Voyages. It is now a boat-based adventure that effectively mixes "it's a small world" with Pirates of the Caribbean to acquaint visitors with the fantastical adventures of Sinbad the sailor, set to Alan Menken's "Compass of Your Heart," composed specifically for this dark ride.

The journey departs from a bustling Arabian village, with its many vendors, musicians, street performers, and other inhabitants wishing Sinbad and his tiger Chandu a safe journey. Just before the boat passes through a tunnel, three village elders warn of stormy weather, and no sooner has the boat left the tunnel does the rain begin. With the wreck of Sinbad's ship in sight, we see he has the good fortune of being rescued by a pair of mermaids.

Sinbad soon gets a new ship and his journey continues as he comes to the aid of the birds of Rukh Island, under siege by a band of pirates attacking them for their magical feathers, which serve as the keys to unlocking the room of treasure that is revealed in the next scene. Rather than take the treasure, Sinbad uses a feather to free an imprisoned giant who had been guarding it, while Chandu subdues one of the pirates. The giant celebrates his newfound freedom with a song, gifting Sinbad with a share of the treasure while the disgruntled pirates look on.

The voyage continues and Sinbad encounters a land overrun by monkeys whose king requests that he use his magic drum to help drive them off. Instead, he befriends the monkeys and with the kingdom at peace, continues on his journey.

Treacherous waters introduce Sinbad to yet another new friend as he and Chandhu mount the back of an enormous whale, which swims them safely to calmer waters.

At last, Sinbad arrives home to the jubilant celebration of his village, and delights in sharing the treasures and gifts received throughout his epic voyage. Fireworks explode against a starlit sky as he enjoys a hero's welcome.

In 2007, this attraction was reintroduced and dramatically retooled from a much different original version, known as Sinbad's Seven Voyages. That version, while it included many similar thematic elements, lacked a cute animal sidekick, unifying theme song, and was considerably darker in tone, with a sense of mystery and unseemliness that did not appeal to guests. While the more menacing giant, mermaids, and perhaps even Sinbad himself as featured in the initial incarnation are remembered fondly by many, it is undeniable that its replacement is more accessible to guests of all ages.

20,000 Leagues Under the Sea: Submarine Voyage
September 4, 2001

Located within Tokyo DisneySea's imposing Mysterious Island, near Journey to the Center of the Earth, this dark ride homage to the classic Jules Verne novel and Walt Disney cinematic adaptation of the same name is a departure from similarly themed attractions at other Disney theme parks around the world, in that the vehicles used in this dark ride do not actually spend any time under water.

We approach the outdoor portion of the queue and enter through a winding spiral staircase overlooking Vulcania Lagoon, where Captain Nemo's *Nautilus* is moored. As we make our way forward, we pass the *Neptune*, a replica of one of the ride vehicles suspended in the air above the lagoon.

The interior portion of the queue passes Captain Nemo's offices and diving equipment, until it reaches the ride vehicles, which are suspended overhead by a track. Up to six passengers may board each vehicle, where they position themselves on a bench in front of a porthole to view the mysteries of the deep.

The attraction's narration is entirely in Japanese. While the vehicles are not submerged in water, the double pane glass of the porthole contains water and a bubble effect to simulate travel beneath the sea.

What is seen beneath the depths is also a departure from other incarnations of this attraction, for once the crew announces its various system checks, confirms that the hatch and airlock have been shut, and begins its dive, Captain Nemo largely hands control of what is seen over to the passengers by letting them know that they can make use of a searchlight to focus in on anything that interests them as their submersible continues its voyage over formations of colorful coral and aquatic plants.

No sooner does the captain extend this invitation do we encounter a ship graveyard known as Kraken Reef, where mysterious creatures of the deep have taken up residence amid ancient wreckage. Blacklight and animatronics mixed with other effects heighten the illusion that we are moving beneath the ocean's depths as we pass a tempting treasure chest, whose last owner is still clinging to it desperately, although it is clear he has long since shuffled off this mortal coil.

An alarm sounds and we see the menacing eye of a giant squid hinting at more dangers to come, as our vehicle is caught within its tentacles. Nemo orders his crew to shock the creature. We manage to escape its grasp, but our submersible begins to rapidly lose power.

We find ourselves in extraordinary peril as we have now entered Lucifer's Trench. The crew reports the supply of oxygen is depleting and even backup power is at dangerously low levels as a final turn takes us through the lost city of Atlantis, where its curious inhabitants peek at us through the ruins.

Captain Nemo orders minimal use of energy, and suddenly an unknown force propels the craft upward. Acting almost as if this is an everyday occurrence, Nemo bids us farewell as we disembark.

The Challenge of Adaptation
How Disney's Imagineers Introduced the Dark Ride to Its First Foreign Audience

Unlike the speed of a roller coaster or the sudden drops of so many thrill rides, the appeal of the dark ride does not originate from the same promise of danger and disorientation. The allure of this type of attraction manifests instead in its mystery, achieved not only through the manipulation of light, but the gradual revelation of the ride's narrative. Disney Imagineers have created a number of dark rides that are not dark in either the literal sense or tonally, with "it's a small world" and Under the Sea ~ Journey Of The Little Mermaid being prime examples.

In these cases, guests are often meant to be transported to a world of fantasy or to another time or place, and the sensory experiences created as a result of the very best of these attractions can have universal appeal.

As has been discussed in the preceding pages, the first Disney theme park to open outside of the United States was Tokyo Disneyland in 1983, which would eventually expand to include Tokyo DisneySea in 2001. In 1992, about an hour outside of Paris, European audiences had their first taste of Euro Disneyland, eventually renamed Disneyland Paris, and a decade later, Walt Disney Studios Park opened as its second gate. Hong Kong Disneyland, to date the smallest park in Disney's global expansion, opened in 2005 in Penny's Bay, Lantau Island, and Shanghai Disneyland opened in the summer of 2016. Each of these parks, though variations on a highly successful theme, would not be without their own unique set of challenges and controversies, owing not only to the partnerships forged to facilitate their creation, but to the cultural differences of their intended audiences.

Disney characters had been a part of Japanese culture ever since the premiere of the 1929 Mickey Mouse short *The Opry House*. World War II and other global conflicts would slow the assimilation, but by the 1950s and 1960s, Japanese children were once again exposed to Disney entertainment. This would play no small part in the appeal of the Disney brand in the years to come as these children grew to have families of their own and wanted their children to enjoy the characters and stories of their youth. Years later, when the potential for Tokyo Disneyland materialized through Disney's partnership with the Oriental Land Company, a Japanese leisure and tourism organization, their intent was to capitalize on exactly this cultural experience. According to William Silvester, in *Building Magic*:

> What OLC had planned from the beginning was that Tokyo Disneyland would be seen from the perspective of an American in Japan and a Japanese view of America.

This plan would depend considerably on the transfer of the long-standing Disney traditions and philosophies to future employees of the company's first international venture. As the park continued to take shape, Silvester wrote, "about 150 people receive[d] the comprehensive training which covered everything from the history of the Disney company to business overviews to technical knowledge." Training was developed by Van Arsdale France, credited for developing the "Disney Way" of training new employees, who prepared himself by learning a great deal about the culture, history, and literature of Japan, only to find that the Japanese wanted an experience just like those in Anaheim and Orlando.

Prior to the park's opening, Disney executive Frank Stanek, who had been instrumental in its realization, told a reporter:

> They know their own culture and they know their own country so well that they really don't believe anyone can do it as good as they know it already and I think to a certain extent they are exactly right, so why try to mingle the two.

However, a degree of mingling was unavoidable, as the Japanese and English languages were blended into attraction signage and show dialogue, and menu options featured a mix of American and Japanese items. Ultimately, the guests, though many of them are native to Japan, are made to feel that they are on vacation in a foreign land.

But how did all of this relate to the adaptation of Disney's various dark rides? Consider Tokyo's version of Pirates of the Caribbean. While similar to its American counterparts in most respects, as the park's Asian financiers insisted on a copy of these revered attractions, Silvester noted that when it came to the ride's boarding process:

> The Japanese do not want to step where people will be sitting, as they consider the bottoms of their shoes to be dirty. Therefore they are inclined to step down to the floor of the boat instead of onto the seat as most guests do in the States, making boarding a slightly more difficult and slower process.

The distinct turns of phrase used by pirates presented another concern, as there were no translations for some of the dark ride's signature dialogue, including "dead men tell no tales." Once again, the mingling of the English and Japanese language tracks would solve this problem, as while the attraction's opening is delivered in Japanese, the audio-animatronic figures speak English and Xavier Atencio's familiar song is also heard in its original language. Guests do not hear Japanese again until they near the end of the attraction, when it is time to disembark the boats.

Critter Country draws consistent crowds with its version of Splash Mountain. While American audiences appreciate the rush of the final drop, because the film that inspired it has long been locked away in the Disney vaults, they may not be as familiar with the backstory as guests are in Japan, where the film is readily available and the ride is one of the park's most popular attractions.

In Fantasyland, guests can also find Pinocchio's Daring Journey, a rare dark ride to open in an overseas Disney theme park before debuting in America. This attraction features Japanese dialogue and is the first in any of Disney's theme parks to to make use of a holographic special effect (used when Lampwick looks at his reflection in a mirror during the ride's Pleasure Island sequence).

Tokyo's Fantasyland also plays host to the Haunted Mansion as stories of ghosts and ghouls have long been popular in Japanese culture. In this attraction, the Ghost Host delivers his disembodied narration in Japanese, but the characters encountered within the dark ride, including Madame Leota, speak in English.

Years later, when it came time to expand, the Oriental Land Company looked to the sea. Resistant to Michael Eisner's ideas for a second gate celebrating motion pictures, they arguably showed a better understanding of theming and the potential for storytelling than the Disney corporate leadership across the globe, noting:

> Japan is an island country surrounded by sea. Historically speaking, cultures were brought to Japan across the seas. The Japanese have a strong love of the sea; you may call it our home.

Here, too, there would be cultural concerns. Disney had proposed a logo for their newly planned theme park featuring a lighthouse, which in American culture symbolized a beacon of hope and the promise of safe return from the stormy seas.

Yet to the Japanese, a lighthouse symbolizes melancholy and loneliness, hardly the most inspirational symbol for a family theme park—especially one where, years earlier, Cinderella Castle was rumored to have been chosen over Sleeping Beauty Castle, as Cinderella's strong work ethic and sense of duty resonated more deeply with the Japanese.

A good deal of Disneyland's original spirit and intent may have been lost in translation with the building of the first international theme park. While Main Street, U.S.A. speaks to visitors of a bygone era in the American parks, Tokyo Disneyland's World Bazaar exists mainly to funnel guests into the park and satisfy their initial impulse to shop. And as the people of Japan, an island nation, may not be familiar with the concept of the American frontier, the park's version of Frontierland was rechristened Westernland, in homage to the American Old West.

As the years passed and Disney opened additional theme parks throughout the world, the lessons learned in Tokyo would prove invaluable. For every new audience the Imagineers wished to connect with, they increasingly understood the need to re-contextualize certain Western and sometimes specifically Disney cultural artifacts in ways that other cultures could engage with on their own terms, from the layout of the park to the many experiences to be encountered within.

Though the Oriental Land Company had insisted early on for exact copies of Disney's most popular attractions, this would not be the case as Disney's expansion continued across the globe. For every new international park to follow, the Imagineers would be faced with the challenge of finding the right balance between making the Disney brand and its blend of imagined reality more familiar to park goers and keeping it unfamiliar and exotic within the context of the culture into which it was assimilating.

CHAPTER SEVEN

Dark Rides in the World of Castles and Kings

Unlike Disney's first effort to expand internationally, where the Japanese knew exactly where they wanted their park, bringing the theme park experience to Europe first required the selection of a suitable location. Disney films had a long history of success in Europe, from the earliest Mickey Mouse cartoons to Walt's repeated forays into live-action films in the United Kingdom following World War II, beginning with *Treasure Island* in 1950. Spurred by the success of Tokyo Disneyland, planning began for European expansion. Over 1,200 locations were being considered for the next Disneyland. Key to Disney's plan was a region with abundant flatland, which would eventually rule out locations throughout Italy and the United Kingdom, and the German habit of vacationing abroad made introducing a park there seem imprudent. Barcelona proved an encouraging possibility, with its favorable climate, airport, railway, hub, and a bustling commercial port, well known to tourists. Eventually, Marne-La-Valée, a site approximately twenty miles east of Paris was chosen. Its central location was accessible by train from Paris, by car and other transportation from throughout France, and by plane for millions of other Europeans.

Despite the familiarity of the European community with the Disney brand, to say that Disney would be welcomed with open arms would be a dramatic overstatement. William Silvester, in *Building Magic*, pointed out that after the initial excitement faded, many families in the area feared the loss of their livelihoods, "not only because the land was to become an American amusement park but because they felt betrayed by their own government for selling them out."

Disney's earliest expansion into the international theme park market had brought with it many valuable lessons. Clearly, as the initial economic struggles of Disneyland Paris would suggest, some divisions of the company would learn how to adapt to their host cultures more quickly than others. Though Disney spent considerable time selecting a site for its European theme park and was conscious of concerns, from the harsh winter weather to how the French treat dogs as if they are members of the family, some in France feared the worst.

As the opening of the park neared in 1992, novelist Jean-Marie Rouart suggested that Euro Disney was symbolic of the ongoing transformation of culture from craft into industry:

> If we do not resist it, the kingdom of profit will create a world that will have all the appearance of civilization and all the savage reality of barbarism.

Another writer was decidedly less worried. Patrick Wajsdman noted:

> France was in trouble if it felt threatened by Mickey Mouse and Donald Duck. A child's laughter has no nationality, no passport, no ideology. Any moment of happiness is there to be enjoyed.

While French intellectuals rushed to criticize Disney's con-tribution to European entertainment, and the people of France pondered whether they might be able to smoke and drink at their leisure within the park as was their custom, and Disney executives created a pricing structure that showed no regard for how the French and Europeans in general went on holiday, the French government, as if in an attempt to both shield them-selves from potential criticism and as a matter of national pride, would insist that Disney pay due respect to French culture in the design of their newest park. The feeling was that Disney's presence in France must be a work of art in its own right, as it would likely be held to the same standard as the great examples of art and architecture found throughout Europe.

Disney's Imagineers understood not only that unlike the Japanese, the French did not want a carbon copy of the American experience, but that so many of their most famous characters and the attractions they inspired—from Peter Pan and Pinocchio to Sleeping Beauty and Snow White—had their roots in European stories and fables.

While this familiarity would allow them to make certain inroads in a park that would ultimately prove to be a microcosm of Europe itself, in other ways it presented new challenges for the designers in creating a world of fantasy that would truly engage these guests in particular. The centerpieces of the Anaheim and Orlando theme parks are majestic castles, both of which drew their inspiration from the European castles of centuries gone by. While this is no doubt enough to instill a sense of wonder in many American park guests, in the land where these castles have stood for ages that same feeling may not be so easy to evoke. The solution, as offered by then president of Imagineering, Marty Sklar, was "to build a castle straight from the storybooks." Le Château de la Belle au Bois Dormant, better known as Sleeping Beauty Castle, features not only elaborate towers and internal pillars carved to resemble giant trees and stained glass windows depicting scenes from its namesake film, but a dungeon that is home to a dragon, which at the time was the largest audio-animatronic that Disney had ever built.

This park's version of Fantasyland would indeed be something of a homecoming for many of Disney's best-known tales. *Cinderella* and *Sleeping Beauty* owe their origins to the fairy tales of French author Charles Perrault, and *Beauty and the Beast* was originally penned by Gabrielle-Suzanne Barbot de Villeneuve in 18th-century Paris. William Silvester explained:

> Here more than in any other land, it was essential to minimize translations on every sign and menu, so Fantasyland was designed to rely on dramatic visual symbols to communicate to guests.

Giving guests the impression that their beloved animated characters had returned home, with traditional dark-ride attractions ranging from Peter Pan's Flight to Pinocchio's

Daring Journey, guests might then follow a path to Discoveryland, this park's take on Tomorrowland.

Designed to commingle fantasy with futurism so as to avoid the potential for obsolescence so often experienced in the earlier incarnations of Tomorrowland, Discoveryland reflects the visions of European thinkers and explorers such as H.G. Wells, Leonardo Da Vinci, and Jules Verne.

In Adventureland, guests encounter Skull Rock and Captain Hook's pirate ship before they see its most iconic attraction, housed inside a battle-worn Spanish fortress: Pirates of the Caribbean. Moving on to Frontierland, guests enter the town of Thunder Mesa, which, as conceived by the Imagineers, is a mining town that sprang up following the success of early settlers who struck gold in the rocks of Big Thunder Mountain. A path up a hill takes us to Phantom Manor, Euro Disney's answer to Haunted Mansion.

In March 2002, following the success of the similarly themed Disney-MGM Studios park in Orlando, Walt Disney Studios Park would open as Paris' second gate. It was around this same time that Euro Disney became known as Disneyland Paris, though it would be more than a decade before Walt Disney Studios Park would see its first dark ride installed. In 2014, based on yet another animated film set in Paris, Ratatouille: The Adventure, a trackless 3D attraction, opened for business, taking guests on a madcap chase through Gusteau's restaurant. In the tradition of Pirates of the Caribbean's Blue Bayou, the ride experience is coupled with Bistrot Chez Rémy, which guests see as they exit the attraction.

For Marty Sklar, Tony Baxter, and the many other Imagineers involved in bringing Disneyland Paris to fruition, both the devil and the delight were in the details. To satisfy potential critics of the Disney aesthetic and to flex their own creative muscles, everything in the park, from the color and texture of the bricks on Main Street, U.S.A. to how they would revisit classic attractions, was in service to the stories being told.

Disneyland Paris' Dark Rides

Blanche Neige et les Sept Nains
April 12, 1992

The Wicked Queen peers down from her castle window above the entrance to this attraction, better known as Snow White and the Seven Dwarfs. Similar to the current Anaheim incarnation of the ride, save for theming in the loading area and the inclusion of a climax more in keeping with the happier resolution of the final Walt Disney World version, this ride ends with Snow White and her prince surrounded by the dwarfs, waving to guests as they make their way to the exit.

"it's a small world"
April 12, 1992

A more refined take on the handcrafted set pieces of the California original, the Paris version of "it's a small world" is also a bit of a departure from the iconic Mary Blair design, though the dolls are still very much a core part of the attraction. Small differences are noticed almost immediately, as passengers ready to take the happiest cruise that ever sailed pass beneath a clock tower where instead of the familiar smiling face, one half depicts the sun and the other shows a sleeping moon.

Entering the show building as a different and more orchestral version of the soundtrack plays, arches, rather than entirely new rooms, separate the scenes, which for the first time include North America with dolls showcasing the United States and Canada, and a Middle Eastern scene with dolls singing in Arabic. As passengers float through the finale, the chorus is heard not only in English, but French and German.

Les Voyages de Pinocchio
April 12, 1992

Save for the use of a French language track and some signage within the ride, this attraction is virtually identical to Pinocchio's Daring Journey in Anaheim.

Peter Pan's Flight
April 12, 1992

This Fantasyland mainstay is nearly identical to the expanded version found in Anaheim, but at approximately three minutes in length, it is slightly longer, and features dialogue spoken in French. The pirate ship ride vehicles are also larger, with a capacity of four passengers each.

Phantom Manor
April 12, 1992

A decidedly darker take on the Haunted Mansion theme than its predecessors, Disneyland Paris' Phantom Manor, located in Frontierland, also offers a more immersive backstory and gives many of the iconic attraction's familiar scenes a Western spin, along with introducing entirely new and unique ride elements.

Another aspect unique to Phantom Manor is that its backstory is closely linked to Thunder Mesa, the mining town that grew in the shadow of Big Thunder Mountain.

The ominous appearance of Phantom Manor, modeled after the Bates' family residence from Alfred Hitchcock's *Psycho*, is less than welcoming. Unlike the American mansions, the exterior of this attraction is not well tended, with weeds and dead trees providing an eerie prelude to what is in store once inside. The manor sits at the top of a hill, overlooking Big Thunder Mountain and a mining colony that has clearly seen better days.

We enter through the front door, which is also unique to Disneyland Paris' take on the attraction, and a cast member ushers us into the foyer. As the door is closed, we are welcomed, in French, by the disembodied narration of the Phantom, who acquaints us with the tale of Ravenswood Manor. As we learn of his fate, which is similar to that of other ghostly narrators, we see the spectral image of one Melanie Ravenswood, appearing and then quickly vanishing from a small mirror in the room. The voice of the Phantom emanates around the room, politely welcoming us, acquainting us with our surroundings, and inviting us to explore the manor further. The face of Melanie Ravenswood, the ghostly bride of this attraction, fades in and out of the smallest mirror during the narration.

We proceed to an adjacent room, which is Phantom Manor's take on the familiar Stretching Room, and then descend to a lower level, where we enter the portrait corridor and make our way toward the loading area. We watch as otherwise nondescript portraits gradually take on a more macabre appearance, and soon we we come upon an oversized portrait of Melanie Ravenswood, dressed in her bridal gown. Turning a corner, we reach the loading area and see a grand staircase leading upward toward a window revealing a relentless storm brewing outside.

Boarding our Doom Buggy, we proceed upward and into blackness, as Melanie, holding a candelabra, helps light our way, bowing as we pass. At this point, those familiar with other versions of the attraction may notice a similarity in its classic soundtrack, but also a distinctly new orchestration.

A suit of armor moves, as if jostled, as we pass to look down what appears to be a seemingly endless hallway with Melanie holding her candelabra, until she disappears, leaving her guiding light suspended in the air. We then see what appears to be a player piano, but keen-eyed riders will notice the shadow of a spirit merrily making the music as a raven perched on a music stand adds its dissonant squawk.

A corridor of doors follows, each of which clearly prevents someone or something from escaping, as screams, shouts, and pounding can be heard from the other side. A large clock is seen next, with its hands rapidly spinning backward, but it is a voice calling out that begins to draw our attention.

In the séance room Madame Leota offers mystic enchantments in both French and English to summon visitors from the spirit realm to a mysterious celebration, which we witness as we pass into the next room, looking down over a balcony.

As guests mingle below, some carrying gifts, others sitting at the long dining table around a stale wedding cake, we see Melanie, standing on a staircase and looking up to the Phantom, who is standing in an open window and laughing at her. Still other spirits twirl about the ballroom dancing to the song being performed on a pipe organ by a ghostly musician, as smaller spirits spring from the pipes.

We next see Melanie, still in her bridal gown, but now seated in her bedroom and weeping in front of a mirror. Moving onward, we pass the Phantom and journey into a graveyard sequence that is much darker than its Haunted Mansion counterparts. The familiar ghostly busts are seen next as they begin to sing "Grim Grinning Ghosts" with the graveyard's other inhabitants joining in.

Our Doom Buggy then takes us through a hole into what appears to be a hint at the terrifying and tragic past of the once prosperous Thunder Mesa. In this twisted take on a ghost town, we see a dilapidated town hall, where its mayor welcomes us and a station master offers us train tickets, before we move deeper into the town's center to witness a shootout, a pharmacist mixing some sort of concoction, and a saloon where a pianist accompanies a showgirl as another spirit tends bar.

Another turn takes us into a dark corridor, lit only by Melanie, now a skeleton, floating in the air with a ghostly glow, directing us to the way out. As we pass through the hall of mirrors, we see the Phantom appear menacingly overhead, before he vanishes and we exit through the manor's wine cellar. Melanie, restored to a more appealing form, pleads with us to hurry back.

Pirates of the Caribbean
April 12, 1992

This incarnation of Pirates of the Caribbean was the last to be updated to include characters from the blockbuster film franchise it inspired. In the summer of 2017, following a renovation coinciding with the park's 25th anniversary, Jack Sparrow was inserted into the attraction and an audio-animatronic Captain Barbossa makes his debut in a scene unique to Disneyland Paris.

Of arguably greater significance were the changes made to some of the attraction's even more iconic characters. The Bride Auction scene was completely overhauled and the comely Redhead, who for half a century has been objectified by lusty, leering buccaneers, is now one herself, holding a rifle as the townspeople surrender their loot to her invading pirate brethren. Similarly revised scenes are planned for Disneyland and Walt Disney World by the end of 2018.

Featuring a significantly different layout than the original attraction, it still includes many of the most iconic scenes. Setting the action within a fortress that has seen its share of battles, the queue begins outside, then winds its way within the fortress, passing the dungeons and overlooking the Blue Lagoon.

The boats leave from a dock near the edge of the fortress and pass beneath an archway out into the lagoon, with the Blue Lagoon restaurant's dining area on one side and a sinister jungle setting on the other. A shipwreck is the first real sign of trouble before the boat begins its ascent into the fortress. We see pirates and soldiers square off in silhouette sword fights behind sails strewn about on either side.

Speaking in French, jailed pirates do their best to coax a key from a mangy guard dog in a familiar scene, before the boats drop down a waterfall right into the middle of a ship's attempt to bombard the fort with cannon fire. Escaping some near hits by both the pirates and the soldiers, we reach the comparative safety of the town, which with few exceptions is a near match to the Disneyland original. Here again, the dialogue is mostly in French, though some English can be heard.

Passing beneath a bridge, we now see the town engulfed in flames, though few in the town seem especially concerned as they share a chorus of "Yo Ho (A Pirate's Life for Me)."

The boat descends again and a ride photo is captured as we emerge, this time in a grotto, where the skeleton pirates guard their treasures. The boat glides into the dock, and we exit.

Buzz Lightyear Laser Blast
April 8, 2006

Very similar to the Disneyland version known as Buzz Lightyear's Astro Blasters, this attraction replaced Le Visionarium, the first Circle-Vision film to feature a narrative and audio-animatronic accompaniment, which closed in 2004. A tribute to the original attraction remains for keen-eyed viewers: look beneath the left arm as you pass Box-o-Bot, and you will see 9-Eye, the Timekeeper's droid assistant.

Walt Disney Studios Park's Dark Rides

Ratatouille: L'Attraction The Adventure
July 10, 2014

Also known as Ratatouille: The Adventure, this trackless, 3D dark ride takes guests on a chaotic excursion through a Parisian restaurant with characters from the 2007 Disney-Pixar film.

Gusteau's restaurant serves as the exterior, Gusteau himself greets us with a brief video introduction, after which we move through a queue styled after the rooftops of Paris. Boarding the ride vehicles, we're shrunken to rat size as Remy and Gusteau deliberate over what meal to serve us. Along with Remy, we fall through the rooftop and into the restaurant's kitchen, where the startled chefs begin to chase us.

After running under tables and carts and stopping for a snack in the cooler, we continue to hide with Remy and Linguini's help, now beneath a stove while the troublesome chef Skinner suspects something is amiss. We follow Remy into the dining area, where Skinner notices us and begins his chase, while Linguini helps us flee into the wall. Skinner grabs at rats and riders menacingly through vents in the walls, but everyone escapes safely to Remy's kitchen to disembark.

Happy Haunts Revisited
Phantom Manor Stakes Its Claim in Thunder Mesa

Perhaps due to its legacy as the origin of so many ghost stories, when it came time to bring the Haunted Mansion to Europe, Imagineers reinvented it from the ground up for the version at Disneyland Paris. Acknowledging that the French were not as receptive to exact duplicates of American attractions as were Japanese audiences, it was also simply a matter of opportunity.

Imagineer Tony Baxter said:

Gothic mansions and graveyards are part of the neighborhood in France—they see them every day. There's nothing exotic or magical about it. We had to do something that would be appealing to that audience.

Baxter, the lead Imagineer on the reinvention of the Haunted Mansion, decided that the most fitting home for the attraction would be in Frontierland, and unlike the ghostly retreats at other Disney parks around the world, the backstory would be indelibly linked to the concept created for its entire land.

This mansion's more rundown appearance is designed to better convey to park guests what lies within. While the Fantasyland setting of Tokyo Disneyland's Haunted Mansion would not have resonated with the new park's European guests in the same way, and Disneyland Paris would not include a Liberty Square or New Orleans Square area like its American counterparts, surely European visitors could identify with the wonder of the American West? The sense of adventure, heroic cowboys, noble Native Americans, and vast expanses of unknown land filled with danger and promise speak to children of all ages.

Speaking of speaking, when plotting a temporary audio track for the attraction, Imagineers used the memorable cackle that closed singer Michael Jackson's *Thriller* music video. Vincent Price would eventually be hired to record an updated version of the Ghost Host's narration, though it was soon discarded in favor of a version performed by the actor Gérard Chevalier, to placate park officials who insisted on French language narration.

With Phantom Manor, much like a number of other attractions throughout Disneyland Paris, it was crucial for the guest experience that what was conveyed through the design of the attraction's exterior and its surrounding environment be made as clear as possible to guests visiting from all over Europe. As Jason Surrell, author of *The Haunted Mansion: Imagineering a Disney Classic*, noted, given the multitude of languages spoken by park guests, "Imagineers needed to visually convey as much story content as possible, relying less on the spoken word."

Within the walls of Phantom Manor, we are told the tale of all of Thunder Mesa and one of its most storied inhabitants, a settler named Henry Ravenswood, who found his fortune in the gold and minerals buried in Thunder Mountain. He would go on to found the Thunder Mesa Mining Company and the surrounding town of Thunder Mesa would thrive as others shared in his success. Surrell explained:

> Thunder Mesa and its outlying regions were inspired by characters and settings originally created for Western River Expedition, a Wild West version of Pirates of the Caribbean that Marc Davis had once developed for the Walt Disney World Magic Kingdom.

As his wealth grew, Ravenswood built a mansion overlooking the town from atop Boot Hill, raised a family, including daughter Melanie, who grew to be a lovely young woman. Though she would attract the attention of many men, a train engineer would one day win her heart, but to the disdain of her father, Melanie's suitor wanted to take her far away from Thunder Mesa.

Gradually, the mine began to yield less and less gold. As miners dug still deeper, hoping for renewed profits, they disturbed the mountain's guardian spirit, the Thunder Bird, who awoke to cause a devastating earthquake, killing both Henry and his wife, Martha.

On the day of the earthquake, while making preparations for her wedding, Melanie's beloved was found dead, mysteriously hanged in the attic of Ravenswood Manor. Unaware, Melanie would spend the rest of her days awaiting his return, dressed in her bridal gown. Yet was she a prisoner of her own broken heart, or of her father's malevolent will? As the years went by, rumors began to swirl among the townspeople. Had Melanie's father killed her fiancé from beyond the grave for daring to take his daughter from him? Has her spirit been trapped within their family home all these years? Most of the residents of Thunder Mesa are far too frightened of the sinister-looking, long-neglected mansion on Boot Hill to go anywhere near it and have taken to calling it Phantom Manor, believing to this day that Melanie remains trapped within its walls waging a ceaseless battle with her father (the eponymous Phantom) and his army of otherworldly associates for the souls of unsuspecting visitors.

CHAPTER EIGHT

Culture in the Dark

Though the Disney company's relationship with China would begin nearly 80 years earlier, when Walt Disney himself visited Shanghai for the Asian premiere of *Snow White and the Seven Dwarfs*, in the wake of the Communist takeover of the country following World War II, the majority of Disney entertainment experienced by Chinese consumers came in the form of lesser knockoffs created by entrepreneurial locals who paid little mind to copyright laws. The company had considered building its second Asian-based theme park in Shanghai as far back as the late 1990s, but Hong Kong Disneyland, located in Penny's Bay, Lantau Island, would open to the public first, on September 12, 2005.

As they had learned from their previous attempts to expand beyond the United States, Disney would approach the construction of its latest theme park with increased care. Unlike those opposed to the opening of Disneyland Paris some years earlier, people in Hong Kong were typically neither intellectuals nor farmers. Describing his first visit to what would become Hong Kong Disneyland, Marty Sklar remembers surveying the scene from the harbor:

> We were warned not to drift too close to the shore, because the small shipyard that was about to be displaced was not thrilled about the coming Disney park. Some of their boat repairmen were reputed to be excellent rifle marksmen.

With the protests surrounding the development of Disneyland Paris still very much on their mind, Disney's executives went to considerable lengths to honor the culture and traditions of the Chinese. Key to their design approach was the practice of feng shui, or creating harmony between people and the surrounding environment. Masters in the practice were employed to make certain the park met with the ancient principles of balance in design, ranging from the placement of the park's gates to the proximity between natural and artificial objects.

Disney's Imagineers had long worked with the understanding that it was this depth of detail that not only elevated their storytelling capabilities, but contributed to the Disney difference—making their contributions to theme park design so much more immersive than those experienced elsewhere. Doris Woodward, Imagineering's creative director at the time, who would go on to lead the development of Shanghai Disneyland a decade later, knew from experience the need "to be sensitive to local culture in our ideas and designs."

Many long-standing Disney theme park traditions are noticeably absent from Hong Kong Disneyland. Specifically, many of the classic dark rides, including Peter Pan's Flight, Alice In Wonderland, Pinocchio's Daring Journey, Splash Mountain, and Pirates of the Caribbean, are missing from what is currently Disney's smallest theme park.

The Dark Rides of Hong Kong Disneyland

Buzz Lightyear's Astro Blasters
September 12, 2005 – August 31, 2017

With a soundtrack presented primarily in English, this version of the Buzz Lightyear dark ride is similar to the Anaheim attraction of the same name.

Hong Kong Disneyland would rescind Buzz Lightyear's commission to Star Command in the summer of 2017 to prepare for an Ant-Man ride planned as part of a major park expansion.

The Many Adventures of Winnie the Pooh
September 12, 2005

Fantasyland's sole dark ride until the opening of "it's a small world" followed three years later, Hong Kong Disneyland's take on Pooh, which is presented in English, combines elements of other versions of the attraction, but most resembles the ride at Walt Disney World's Magic Kingdom.

"it's a small world"
April 28, 2008

Hong Kong Disneyland's version of this classic attraction was the first to open with Disney characters rendered in the Mary Blair style and placed into the scenes appropriate to their stories. The iconic song is sung in Cantonese, English, Korean, and Tagalog. It also includes an extended sequence set in Asia, a rainforest segment, a new scene for North America, and a room highlighting the Middle East. The final room features fiber-optic lighting effects unique to Hong Kong's version of the ride.

Mystic Manor
May 17, 2013

Hong Kong Disneyland's answer to the ever popular Haunted Mansion attraction, Mystic Manor is a haunted house-themed dark ride located in the Mystic Point section of the park. Due to differences in Chinese culture, the ghostly inhabitants of its iconic precursor have been replaced by enchantments witnessed by passengers who make their way through the many rooms of a Victorian-style mansion.

As we make our way through the queue, we come across a portrait of Lord Henry Mystic and his pet monkey, Albert, and then gather for the usual pre-show, though here it is a light-hearted slideshow presentation narrated by Lord Mystic, who describes the various rooms throughout Mystic Manor and the highlights of his many collections, while an audio-animatronic Albert makes several appearances. As we learn more about this curious dwelling, Lord Mystic cautions us about an enchanted music box full of rare and powerful magic that can bring inanimate objects to life. His narration is in English, though some Chinese can be heard spoken throughout the attraction and in the lyrics to the ride's music.

We then make our way to the loading area and board a ride vehicle to begin the tour. Like Pooh's Hunny Hunt at Tokyo Disneyland, this attraction features a trackless system, meaning that each rider's experience can be different each time.

We first find ourselves in the Acquisitions and Cataloging Room, where many of the assorted artifacts that Lord Mystic has accumulated in his travels still await documentation and placement on the shelves. He is searching for Albert, but mentions the music box, which is visible in the room, before leaving to continue his search.

Albert then appears and unlocks the music box, unleashing a trail of magic dust that floats through the air and enchants many of the antiquities in the room. From here, we travel to the Music Room. As we move around the centerpiece of a large piano, many different musical instruments begin to play as the magic dust works its enchantment. Albert sits atop an enormous pipe organ watching the action unfold while we move on to the Solarium, where he feeds one Venus Flytrap as another tries to bite us. Suddenly, the room turns black as night.

Moving on, we enter a chamber with a painting of a Nordic god who comes to life and blows a gust of icy wind through the room that shatters a mirror. Next, in Mediterranean Antiquities, we watch the scene of a gladiator facing a lion comes to life on the side of a ceramic jar and a portrait of a woman transforms into the head of Medusa, much like the changing portraits of the Haunted Mansion.

The tour will also take us to the Armory, where Albert has found himself inside a cannon, as a samurai tries repeatedly to behead him. Another cannon opens fire, sending the ride vehicle off toward singing suits of armor, and it continues onward, only to encounter a crossbow, which takes aim just as we move to the next room.

Here, we find ourselves among a collection of Egyptian artifacts. A sarcophagus standing upright radiates a green glow before a swarm of insects emerges from it, blocking out all light in the room as we blindly navigate to a collection of Tribal Arts. A Tiki figure with emerald green eyes spews lava from its mouth. The other Tiki statues come to life, some pounding drums in time with the music, while others have a more menacing purpose, aiming blow guns at Albert, who is pinned to the wall by their darts.

The vehicles next proceed into a room where a giant statue of a Monkey King becomes bewitched and uses its staff to summon a storm, causing the room to spin wildly and the many paintings and tapestries adorning the walls to tear apart and fall to pieces.

Albert appears and the enchanted statue attempts to strike him with a bolt of lightning, but instead obliterates a portion of the wall. Desperately clinging to an enchanted harp, Albert catches hold of the music box as it passes by in the storm, and succeeds in closing it, sealing the magic within, and the ride vehicles abruptly return to the Acquisitions and Cataloging Room.

Albert sighs with relief and Lord Mystic appears, just as all has been put to right, asking whether Albert had touched the music box, as the legends just might be true after all. Albert denies any such mischief and Lord Mystic bids his guests farewell as the ride carriages move to the unloading area.

Another Take on the Classic Haunted House Dark Ride

Though the park would open lacking many of the iconic dark rides that so many years before had helped Walt Disney set the standard for theme park entertainment, at the grand opening of Mystic Point on May 17, 2013, Bill Ernst, president and managing director of Asia Parks and Resorts, seemed confident that Mystic Manor would rank among Disney's most innovative and compelling dark rides:

> For the first time, guests can immerse themselves in a unique adventure of theatrical wonders that combines

traditional storytelling with innovative technology and special effects.

Like Disney's French partners, those involved in the planning of Hong Kong Disneyland did not want a carbon copy of everything that came before. Breaking new ground meant bragging rights in the increasingly competitive recreation industry. Acknowledging the absence of dark rides in the park, Disney's designers looked to the Haunted Mansion for inspiration. Unlike Tokyo, however, a simple transplant of the American version would not suffice. Jason Surrell, in *The Haunted Mansion: Imagineering a Disney Classic*, reports concept designer Robert Coltrin as having said:

> The Haunted Mansion is a magic show. It's Yale Gracey tinkering with little things, but at the end of the day, it's a show where we can show off a bunch of really great illusions.

There would be no Doom Buggies escorting guests through this attraction. Instead, the chosen trackless ride system takes six passenger vehicles through the ride, allowing Imagineers not only greater control over what guests see at any point during their experience, but the ability to isolate and rejoin them as the story requires, offering significantly more scare potential for an attraction themed around the supernatural.

Recognizing that Chinese audiences do not view ghosts and the afterlife in the same way as Americans and Europeans do, Joe Lanzisero, the Imagineer in charge of the expansion project, who had also been a creative lead for the Tokyo Disney Resort, agreed:

> The Chinese have a very different relationship with the afterlife. Singing happy ghosts would not have the same effect there.

Indeed, the Chinese feel that while the spirits of the deceased should be revered and respected, care should also be taken to avoid them—not necessarily a promising premise for a theme park interested in attracting guests.

Years earlier, when creating the backstory for Tokyo DisneySea's version of Tower of Terror, Lanzisero developed a character named Harrison Hightower, an affluent traveler and adventurer who collected rare artifacts from around the world. As a member of the Society of Explorers and Adventurers, he would later boast of his exploits bringing back an African idol that some said was cursed. He dismissed the curse as nonsense, but would soon find out otherwise, when he entered the elevator of his hotel carrying the idol, never again to leave. Lanzisero and his design team felt that another member of S.E.A. could serve as the inspiration for the attraction being planned for Hong Kong.

This gave life to Lord Henry Mystic, his name serving the dual purpose of identifying him as a new and entirely unique character and hinting to guests at what the attraction might have in store for them. Also serving a dual purpose would be Albert, who as Lord Mystic's playful monkey sidekick sets the events of the dark ride into motion. In conceiving Albert, Coltrin noted:

> In the Chinese culture, a monkey represents mischievousness, and in a ride where you have so little time to explain things, you see a monkey as someone who will get into trouble.

And that is exactly what transpires. As Lord Henry welcomes us for a tour through his home, Mystic Manor, which doubles as a museum of art and antiquities, Albert opens one of his master's latest finds: a mysterious music box, said to have the power to bring inanimate objects to life. While a melody does emanate from the music box with Albert's touch, so too does a magical energy, which proceeds to enchant everything it touches.

As music composed by Danny Elfman serves as the soundtrack to the impending mayhem, guests follow Albert onboard their Mystic Magneto Electric Carriages from room to room throughout the manor, as more and more objects become enchanted and seemingly turn on him. Albert finds himself in increasingly greater danger until a statue of the Monkey King summons a supernatural tornado that rips apart the house until he can shut the lid of the music box and seal its enchantment within. Instantaneously, guests are returned where their tour began, where Lord Mystic, oblivious to what has just transpired, once again cautions Albert to not touch the music box.

For all its incredible innovation and effects, what makes Mystic Manor so enjoyable as a dark ride differs little from the countless examples that came before it, in attractions such as Pirates of the Caribbean, and of course, its most direct ancestor, the Haunted Mansion. Lanzisero, Coltrin, and their design team wanted characters and designs similar to those created by Marc Davis. Like those classic attractions, the thrill of fear is delivered with a wink, every scare offset with a smile. Lanzisero said, about the lighter touch Davis brought to these earlier dark rides:

> With a believable environment, people are drawn in and can then be engaged by the story—and its scare factor. Characters [can be] highly caricatured in their look, but the environments they live in are still pretty grounded in the real world.

That design philosophy would extend to the outward look of Mystic Manor, which is at once grounded in the reality established by its surroundings and introduces guests to its more cartoonish inhabitants.

This balance of the exaggerated and the exact would also facilitate how Disney would communicate with its diverse range of park visitors. Albert's eyes and other oversized features help guests understand what he is experiencing immediately. Guests touring through Mystic Manor are able to witness its story unfold largely devoid of any dialogue. Lanzisero elaborates:

> One of the big lessons from Marc and the original Imagineers, many of whom came from film and animation, was their ability to communicate emotions quickly, and that was usually done through caricature.

Stepping into Darkness
Walking Through Hong Kong Disneyland's Nightmare Experiment

If Walt Disney's original plans to make the now classic dark ride attractions Pirates of the Caribbean and Haunted

Mansion walk-throughs had come off as intended, would they be as popular with audiences as they are today? While that is difficult to speculate, the proliferation of walk-through experiences designed to engage and sometimes frighten guests since Disneyland's 1955 opening is undeniable.

Amusement parks around the world offer walk-through attractions, typically during the Halloween season. Universal Studios parks around the world are themed each year for Halloween Horror Nights, featuring terrifying mazes, attraction overlays, and live performers interacting with park guests in place of traditional audio-animatronics. Knott's Berry Farm, one of Disneyland's earliest competitors in southern California, transforms itself each fall into Knott's Scary Farm, with several different scare zones and the dead and undead running amok.

So perhaps it was only natural that a Disney theme park explores the darker side of some of its own legacy and revisits what might have been.

Offered for the first time in the fall of 2016, in Hong Kong Disneyland's Pavilion, guests assembled in the lobby outside of the Royal Laboratory for the Scientific Study of Phantasmagorian Phenomena. An attendant dressed in medical attire ushered them into a steam-punk style laboratory, where they were greeted by a professor who did not appear to be entirely human. The professor opened a large circular door that offers to transport visitors to some of Disney's most sinister and unsettling realms.

Guests brave enough to pass through the door into this nightmarish world found themselves deep in the Louisiana bayou, where they were greeted by a woman carrying a lantern who escorted them to a small hut where Dr. Facilier, from *The Princess and the Frog*, performed a vaudevillian voodoo show. Dr. Facilier began to summon his friends from the other side and a demonic black clad figure appeared. The doctor hid behind a cloth, and when the mysterious figure pulled it away, he vanished.

Guests progressed deeper into the nightmare, following the skeletal likeness of a seemingly familiar buccaneer into the dimly lit dungeons from Pirates of the Caribbean, where within each cell were the remains of a long-dead pirate. As "dead men tell no tales" echoed in the darkness of the dungeon chamber, Jack Sparrow led guests into a passageway and the next phase of their nightmare.

Finding themselves in the bedroom of Sid Phillips, the menacing neighbor kid from *Toy Story*, guests soon noticed that they were surrounded by his collection of mutant toys. The melody of a jack-in-the-box revealed an enormous hand, and Babyface appeared from the shadows. The room filled with flashing lights as a six-armed doll with a sewn-together head and mismatched eyes began dancing about and interacting with guests until the White Rabbit from Tim Burton's *Alice In Wonderland* appeared to lead them through a dark forest to the Mad Hatter, imprisoned in an asylum with one of the Red Queen's guards standing watch. Through the windows, visitors saw that the Mad Hatter was hosting a tea party in his cell to a guest list of headless figures. Curiously, each of his guests had a red scarf around their neck. The hatter emerged from his cell and selected one of the new arrivals to join him, seated them at the head of the table, and placed a red scarf around their neck. As he reached for a large pair of shears, blood red curtains covered the windows and the guard urged the guests to move on. All but one, at any rate.

Wandering through a hedge maze, guests were startled by ghosts and gargoyles that menacingly emerged from the darkness. Escaping from the maze into the professor's laboratory, guests crossed over a catwalk and watched scenes featuring some of Disney's many animated villains on screens placed on either side. The professor's assistant appeared, moving them onward, and the professor was seen one last time, working at his machinery and wishing guests well as they exited.

Would an attraction like this be welcomed by audiences in other Disney parks? Would it be considered outside of Hong Kong, given Disney's long-standing concerns with capacity? While there are certainly any number of walk-through success stories, only time will tell if Disney adopts it on a wider scale.

CHAPTER NINE

Bringing Magic to the Mainland

Disney would open its fourth international theme park destination in an area where it had already spent a considerable amount of time investing in its awareness of the history and culture of the host nation. Roughly a two-hour flight from its sister park in Hong Kong, Shanghai Disneyland opened its gates in the city's Pudong district on June 16, 2016.

As with Hong Kong Disneyland before it, the prelude to Disney's eventual foothold in China had been stymied by decades of politics, piracy, and other problems well beyond even its considerable sphere of influence. It was not until the mid-1980s that Disney programs were allowed to air on Chinese television with episodes of the Mickey and Donald cartoon series. Not only would the program and its characters reach the youth of China in the same way that Snow White had decades earlier, they convinced the future mayor of Shanghai that a Disneyland-style park in his city would be a phenomenal success.

Far from an overnight process, construction on the park did not begin until 2011. Planned as its centerpiece was the Enchanted Storybook Castle. Not home to any single princess, it was instead conceived as something of a timeshare for Disney's entire royal family. The park would come to feature a number of other distinctions from its forerunners, both in the United States and abroad. Mickey Avenue replaces Main Street, U.S.A. as the entryway to adventure, and the pirate-themed Treasure Cove and similarly unique Gardens of Imagination are both all-new experiences. Gardens of Adventure speaks directly to the Chinese peoples' traditional love of gardens, with Garden of the Twelve Friends paying homage to both the twelve signs of the Chinese zodiac and popular Disney and Pixar characters depicted as mosaics within view of a garden of cherry blossoms. According to William Silvester, in *Building the Magic*:

> It was intended that the Garden of Twelve Friends would enable guests to experience a blend of Disney storytelling with traditional Chinese elements and pays homage to the central role of the Chinese zodiac in daily life in China.

In designing the park, Imagineer Xuan Yu reveals that thousands of Chinese citizens suggested they have similar interests to Disney theme park visitors around the world. Silvester continued:

> One key thing we have found is that they all want to take away from their Shanghai Disney Resort experience a collective memory that can be shared among family members throughout their entire lives.

The Dark Rides of Shanghai Disneyland

Buzz Lightyear Planet Rescue
June 16, 2016

The latest generation of Buzz Lightyear's intergalactic adventures still sees the space ranger squaring off against the Evil Emperor Zurg, but bases much of its action on the opening scene of *Toy Story 2* and the location of Zurg's fortress planet, as Star Command recruits take on his Sentry Bots and attempt to destroy his Super Blaster weapon. The audio for this attraction is presented in Chinese.

Disney's Imagineers have incorporated screen animation into this incarnation of the popular interactive dark ride, bringing Buzz himself more into the action than ever before.

The Many Adventures of Winnie the Pooh
June 16, 2016

Like Hong Kong Disneyland, this version of Pooh combines Disney's previous journeys through the Hundred Acre Wood, though it too most closely mirrors the Magic Kingdom attraction, except the ride's audio component is presented in Chinese.

Peter Pan's Flight
June 16, 2016

Shanghai Disneyland's take on Peter Pan's Flight offers a mix of the classic audio-animatronic and fiber optic effects combined with CG and screen animation to enhance the narrative of the experience in a way that remains faithful to the original attraction. The result is a longer and more immersive ride, which should delight many fans of the film and those who have long enjoyed the Disneyland original. The language track is in Chinese, while the music is taken from the film. The galleon ride vehicles are also slightly larger than their earlier counterparts, accommodating one or two more passengers each.

Taking off from Kensington Gardens, we see Tinker Bell narrowly avoid being made dinner by a hungry frog as our ship passes through London's Bloomsbury neighborhood.

Peter Pan appears from the shadow of the starlit sky and we come upon a scene in the Darling nursery, where he is teaching the children to fly to the tune of "Second Star to the Right," using Tinker Bell's pixie dust to send them skyward to London, as their nursemaid, Nana, helplessly waves a paw goodbye.

Flying over London landmarks, such as Big Ben, Peter leads Wendy, Michael, and John off to Neverland, with Skull Rock, the Indian encampment, and the *Jolly Roger* in view below.

A splash landing inside Skull Rock reveals that Tinker Bell has been taken prisoner by the villainous Captain Hook, who is sneaking up on Peter Pan. We next see the Darling children captive aboard the *Jolly Roger* as Peter duels with Hook and the hungry crocodile waits below for his next meal.

Hook falls into the waiting jaws of the crocodile while Mr. Smee desperately tries to save him as Peter Pan crows above.

With Peter victorious over the pirates, Tinker Bell sprinkles her pixie dust over the *Jolly Roger* and the Darling children return home to London, the clock face of Big Ben opening as the galleon pulls into port and we disembark.

Pirates of the Caribbean: Battle for the Sunken Treasure
June 16, 2016

Launching from within an abandoned fortress of the Royal Navy where Barbosa's Bounty restaurant takes the place of Disneyland's Blue Bayou, we board updated boats and set sail into the lagoon. A talking skull warns of danger ahead as we pass through a cave and into a grotto to come upon many seemingly familiar scenes, including one of imprisoned pirates who had been trying to coax the key to their cell from the guard dog for so long that they all died.

Rounding the bend, another skeleton standing at the helm of a marooned ship is suddenly struck by a surge of lightning, which after coursing through its bony figure, gives life to none other than Captain Jack Sparrow. It now becomes clear that this is something more than the traditional take on Disney's classic pirate attraction. It is the first time the characters of the hit film franchise have directly inspired a new dark ride adventure, and here the wily captain enlists riders as crew in his attempt to recover the lost treasure of Davy Jones hidden somewhere beneath the murky sea.

Mixing Disney's storytelling expertise with the state-of-the-art technologies perfected by Imagineers, we are then made to feel as if we are swallowed by the ocean, plummeting to a graveyard of lost ships where pirates busily plunder the gold from rotting hulls. The boat rouses the beastly Kraken and then seeks refuge within the remains of Davy Jones' battered ship.

Sailing next to mermaid territory, we encounter two winsome sirens and follow a path of glittering treasure, before a hammer-faced crewmember of Davy Jones' ship appears to inform us that "the captain be wantin' a word with with ye!" Moving through a cavern, we hear a propulsive, yet melancholy tune being played on an organ and soon see that the instrumentalist is none other than Davy Jones, who it is clear will not be giving up his riches so easily.

A fleet of ships rises to the surface and we are caught in the middle as both sides fight over the fate of the treasure. Cannons fire above and below as one by one ships are blasted back beneath the sea and we soon find ourselves trapped inside the hull of a badly damaged vessel.

With water rushing in from all sides, Davy Jones takes up arms against Jack Sparrow, who has been hoarding what he can of the treasure on board a row boat. Just as Jack loses his sword, he swings to safety, momentarily out of reach of Jones' deadly blade, and aims a cannon in his direction. Though he misses, he creates a hole in the ship, unleashing a massive rush of water that sets his own boat free in the current and propels us backwards while Davy Jones is lost in the waves.

We next see Captain Jack's rowboat washed upon the shore, where he stands with his newly acquired riches. But does Davy Jones have one last curse in store? The boats turn a final corner and move up an incline before reaching the dock to unload.

Another Step Forward
The Enchanted Storybook Castle Walk-Through

Disney's majestic castles have always been the centerpiece of their respective theme parks. From Sleeping Beauty's wondrous realm in Disneyland to Disney's latest offering in Shanghai, each castle is not only a gateway to the world of fantasy and imagination, but often an opportunity to experience the stories associated with the castle's resident princess.

Beginning with dioramas created in the style of Eyvind Earle's memorable production design nearly two years after its opening, guests at Disneyland could relive the story of Princess Aurora as they meandered through the castle at their own pace. And though the technology would evolve considerably, nearly forty years later a similar experience was made available at Disneyland Paris. In Tokyo Disneyland, guests are invited to explore the castle of Cinderella and Prince Charming, where they will find paintings, dioramas, and other works of art that share their story, as well as the legendary glass slipper.

While Shanghai Disneyland's Enchanted Storybook Castle belongs to no single princess, its high-tech walk-through experience, Once Upon a Time Adventure, invites us to relive the story of *Snow White and the Seven Dwarfs*. After a cast member awakens the Magic Mirror, it sets the stage for what is to come by introducing us to Snow White, Prince Charming, the dwarfs, and the jealous queen.

The Magic Mirror transforms into a portal that lets us enter the world of Snow White, as her story is brought to life through a combination of tangible set pieces, audio-animatronics and special effects, and computer-generated imagery. We interact with her forest friends before arriving in the queen's secret chamber, where we find a cauldron brewing. It is not long before the queen herself arrives and summons some dark magic from the bubbling brew. She transforms herself to the malevolent old hag and reveals her poisoned apple before disappearing in an ominous bolt of lightning.

The next scene is in the relative comfort of the Dwarfs' woodland cottage—that is, until the queen arrives in her disguise and tempts Snow White with an apple.

We next see the prince, desperate to revive Snow White, kneeling at her forest pyre to kiss her. With true love's kiss, the wicked queen's spell is broken. Snow White awakens to find the embrace of her prince and her dwarf companions keeping faithful vigil, with her future secure in the warm glow of the castle in the distance.

While not a ride, this attraction, much like Hong Kong Disneyland's Nightmare Experiment, uses a combination of familiar Disney characters, lighting, effects, music, and a story to create an immersive experience in much the same way Imagineers design more traditional dark rides. With the closure of Snow White's Scary Adventures in Disney World as part of the Fantasyland expansion project, it is encouraging that Disney's creative team can look to its original princess for inspiration more than eighty years after her cinematic debut and still find new ways to innovate and engage with their audience.

CHAPTER TEN

The Dark Ride Genre Outside of Disney

Walt Disney, with the help of Imagineers and design partners such as Arrow Development, defined the dark ride with Disneyland and the parks to follow around the globe, using the experience as both a storytelling medium and a means of entertainment, but other innovators would emerge. Some would be inspired by the more family-oriented example set by the Disney theme park experience, and others, like Bill Tracy, would go in a decidedly different direction. In only fifteen years working in the dark ride genre, Tracy would be responsible for the design of approximately eighty different attractions.

Born in Toledo, Ohio, in 1916, Bill Tracy was the son of devout Methodists. He would develop interests contrary to his religious upbringing, visiting both an insane asylum and a graveyard (with the desire to wake the dead) while still in his teens. He began his professional career in 1952 and before long became art director for Ringling Bros. and Barnum and Bailey Circus, in Sarasota, Florida, before contracting with Macy's to create floats and window displays for their annual Thanksgiving Day Parade in New York City.

In the 1960s, Tracy's work would transition from family-friendly holiday displays and circus props to something altogether different. He had already been doing freelance design for dark ride manufacturers, including the Pretzel Amusement Ride Company. His earliest known dark ride was the Jungeland boat ride in Wildwood, New Jersey, which took passengers through tropical scenes of monkeys, snakes, a charging rhinoceros, and even cannibals, until it closed in 1989. According to the BillTracyProject website:

> After contracting work with Pretzel and learning about the dark ride industry, Bill decided to take control of the "dark side" of the amusement park industry by starting his own company designing and building dark rides. Now that he was a direct competitor to Pretzel, the company that used to hire him, he knew he had to offer something new and exciting that the industry had never seen before and push the creativity and realism of dark rides to a new level.

Additional attractions would soon follow, and Tracy formed his first dark ride company, Outdoor Dimensional Display Co., using many of the same techniques he had explored in the design and building of his floats and displays earlier in his career.

With his dark rides taking an average of only a few months to build, Tracy's business expanded to offer the re-theming of existing dark rides so that amusement park operators could keep their attractions fresh amid industry competition.

Much like Disney's Imagineers, Tracy understood the importance of the theming of his dark rides, both inside and out, and would go to great lengths to decorate his attractions:

> The façade was the marketing and advertisement for the ride and hopefully lured a person to use some of their precious ride tickets on that particular attraction.

Within the rides, guests generally witnessed scenes far more gruesome, sexual, and violent than anything experienced in a Disney attraction, with women often being subjected to torture or other unsettling situations.

Financial troubles led Tracy to partner with the New Jersey-based Universal Design Limited. Through them he designed a number of additional dark rides, including Ghost Ship, in Ocean City Maryland, and Miracle Strip Amusement Park's Hour 13, which in Tracy's tradition was "replete with skulls, skeletons and mummies, and with a sprinkling of sex appeal."

As the needs of his business grew, Tracy would collaborate with yet another company to help finance the expansion of his dark ride interests. In 1966, he partnered with Messmore and Damon to create Amusement Display Associates, and would launch, among other things, the new Hush Puppy ride system. Exclusively available through his company, "the Hush-Puppy was the most versatile dark ride system to date and was able to negotiate tight turns, roller-coaster-like dips, wave rooms, tilted rooms, and steep grades," making it ideal for a multitude of attractions.

During his tenure at Amusement Displays, Tracy would also design Kennywood Park's Ghost Ship, one of his best-known dark rides. Similar in name only to its Ocean City predecessor, this Pittsburgh, Pennsylvania, attraction took passengers through a labyrinthine world of pirates, skeletons, and sea creatures, before it was lost to a fire in 1975.

Like Disney's Imagineers, Tracy used techniques including blacklight paint, forced perspective, lighting effects, and optical illusions to stage the scenes for his attractions. While he often went to great lengths in terms of theming, there was usually no narrative structure to speak of in his dark rides, and the various themes of pirates or lunatic asylums only supported the often gruesome scenes and effects witnessed by guests throughout the experience.

Tracy's rides would go on to terrify and excite park goers up and down the East Coast for several decades, until he died of heart disease in 1974, at 58. His company would continue on through a series of new names and changes in ownership and the majority of his attractions would close, either gradually falling into disrepair or becoming obsolete and the victims of continued industry innovation.

Today, Waldameer Park, located in Erie, Pennsylvania, still plays host to both one of Tracy's surviving Whacky Shack dark rides and a Pirates Cove walk-through attraction he designed, and examples of his Haunted House dark rides can still be found in Camden Park in West Virginia and Ocean City, Maryland.

Though Bill Tracy and Walt Disney could not have been further apart in their design aesthetic, both men helped define the genre of the dark ride and in their own way flourished in an industry that is in need of constant innovation and revitalization. While only a fraction of Tracy's attractions remain in operation today, their survival is a testament to not only his skill as a designer, but to their ability to frighten, delight, and engage park goers in ways that countless others in his field would emulate.

So just what has the inspiration of dark ride designers Walt Disney and his Imagineers and Bill Tracy brought to the field of themed entertainment since their pioneering efforts over sixty years ago? The following is a list of ten standout attractions from around the world that through a clever combination of sets, sounds, lighting, effects, and motion immerse guests in an entirely new world to tell a story and communicate ideas that ignite our emotions and inspire our intellect and imagination.

The Amazing Adventures of Spider-Man
Universal Studios: Orlando (May 28, 1999)

This 3D dark ride takes guests on an adventure unlike any other through the streets of New York City, as they watch Spider-Man face off against some of the most dangerous villains in his rogues' gallery. The queue begins in the offices of *The Daily Bugle*, where we become on-the-spot reporters before boarding our ride vehicles as J. Jonah Jameson sends us out in search of a headline-worthy scoop. No sooner do we drive through one of New York's back alleys do we come face to face with Spider-Man, who warns us that Doctor Octopus is loose in the city and that spells trouble. Along with Electro, Hydro-Man, Scream, and the Hobgoblin, he has used an anti-gravity cannon to hijack the Statue of Liberty.

Strobe lights, fog, heat, and other effects are blended spectacularly with the attraction's use of video imagery as we repeatedly find ourselves in harm's way.

As the ride nears its end, Doc Ock blasts the vehicle with his anti-gravity cannon, raising it several hundred feet into the air. He releases it into a deadly freefall. Just when it seems all hope is lost, Spider-Man spins a web to catch the vehicle and we see that he's captured all of the villains.

The attraction's massive popularity led to a re-creation being built for Universal Studios Japan in 2004.

Atlantis Adventure
Europa-Park: Rust, Baden Württemberg, Germany (2007)

Found in Germany's largest theme park, and similar to Disney's Buzz Lightyear series of attractions, Atlantis Adventure takes us on a simulated underwater journey to the fabled lost city of Atlantis, where we fire lasers at seemingly peaceful aquatic life while cheerful music plays. The richly detailed ocean environment features a coral reef and volcano along with animatronic sharks, turtles, crustaceans, and other staples of sea life, before things take a more fanciful turn and we dodge moving anchors and encounter pirate skeletons and giant sea horses as we travel through the sunken ruins of the once-prosperous city until ending in a treasure chamber.

Carnival Festival
Efteling World of Wonders: Kaatsheuvel, Netherlands (1984)

The land-based Dutch answer to "it's a small world" features vehicles run over a track, carnival-style music in place of the charming song by the Sherman Brothers, and caricatured animatronic figures that border on offensive. Though primarily focusing on Europe, the attraction visits a number of other countries and regions, including China, Japan, Mexico, Africa, and the Arctic.

Curse of Darkastle
Busch Gardens: Williamsburg, Virginia (May 1, 2005)

The backstory details the macabre history of the cursed castle's long-ago inhabitant, Prince Ludwig, who as a neglected child shared a fateful encounter with a mysterious old woman one winter's night that would forever alter his destiny. Ludwig would learn that this was no ordinary woman, but a werewolf who had the gift of prophecy. She told him that he would one day rule the kingdom into darkness and corruption. Her premonition drives the young prince mad. As the years passed and his fate as foretold became a reality, he turned the castle into a fortress, intent on securing his rule. His royal advisors would try to overthrow him, but laughing off their threat, he instead invited them to a celebration in their honor, taking them on a tour of his castle in a company of golden sleighs. The next morning, while the sleighs were all accounted for, Ludwig and his guests were nowhere to be found.

Motion-simulator vehicles take us through the ruined castle as the story unfolds with a mix of physical sets, projected images, and special effects. One of the first things we see is the spirit of Ludwig's mother, who warns us to flee outside the castle's walls, for her son has no power there.

But this tour is preordained and Ludwig beckons, his ghost threatening and menacing us as we make our way through the castle's many rooms. In the music room, Ludwig raises instruments into the air and slams them around the ride vehicles. In the kitchen, he hurls knives.

As we enter the library, the ghost of Ludwig's mother appears once again and pulls the ride vehicle up through the fireplace, wrestling with her son in an attempt to pull it outside of the castle's walls to safety. In a final attempt to attack us, Ludwig leaves the castle, but in the process, he loses his soul and turns to ice, shattering to pieces. We're splashed with water as his final threats echo in the distance and we disembark.

Dreamflight
Efteling World of Wonders: Kaatsheuvel, Netherlands (1993)

The largest theme park in the Netherlands features this attraction combining ancient myth, legend, and folklore. Using an overhead track similar to Peter Pan's Flight, we begin our journey in a magical mountain kingdom with a flowing waterfall and then move on to a forest glen populated by talking trees and piskies.

The voyage continues through a blossoming garden where fairies ride swings and gather flowers by the riverside until we are ushered forward through a starlit tunnel into a realm of castles in the sky, before returning to earth and mingling with gnomes and trolls in a marshland setting.

The Flying Trunk
Tivoli Gardens: Copenhagen, Denmark (1993)

A celebration of the stories of Hans Christian Anderson, the Flying Trunk takes us on a trip through thirty-two animatronic scenes depicting classic tales such as "The Little Mermaid," "The Tin Soldier," "The Ugly Duckling," and "The Emperor's New Clothes," aboard trunk-shaped vehicles.

Harry Potter and the Forbidden Journey
Universal Studios: Orlando, Florida (June 18, 2010)

Revitalizing theme park entertainment in much the same way J.K. Rowling's novels inspired countless children to rediscover the joy of reading, the Wizarding World of Harry Potter opened at Universal Orlando's Islands of Adventure in the summer of 2010 with this as its marquee attraction. The queue begins deep beneath the castle in its dungeons, twists up through the greenhouse and back into the castle, winding through the Portrait Room, Gryffindor Common Room, Headmaster's Office, and other familiar settings, as part of a tour of Hogwarts, with appearances by Professor Dumbledore, as well as Harry, Ron, and Hermione, along the way.

After a safety warning from the Sorting Hat, we enter the Room of Requirement and board the ride vehicle, a bench that Hermione enchants with Floo Powder and then tells us to say "Observatory" to start our trip. Flying out through one of the Observatory's arches, we follow Harry, Ron, and Hermione to watch a Quidditch match, before encountering Hagrid, who asks us whether we have seen his Hungarian Horntail. An animatronic version of the dragon unleashes his fiery breath.

Fleeing the immediate danger, we press on to the Forbidden Forest, where we meet Aragog. With Hermione's help, we evade his deadly venom, but the Whomping Willow sends us hurtling back toward the Quidditch pitch, where Gryffindor's latest match with Slytherin is interrupted by the unwelcome presence of Dementors.

Harry attempts to lead our escape, but we instead find ourselves in the Chamber of Secrets, with the Dementors still in pursuit. Lord Voldemort's Dark Mark rises from the skeleton of the long dead Basilisk and we are somehow drawn into the mouth of the ancient statue of Salazar Slytherin. An icy chill fills the room as Dementors emerge to suck out our souls, but Harry is able to repel them with his Patronus Charm.

We make our final escape over the Black Lake to the safety of Hogwarts, where a cheering crowd of students awaits our return in the Great Hall. Professor Dumbledore congratulates us on our bravery and tells us we are free to return to Hogwarts at any time.

The extraordinary success of this attraction and its accompanying themed land was soon duplicated at Universal Studios Japan in July 2014 and in Universal Studios Hollywood in April 2016. In addition to its rich theming and groundbreaking special effects, Harry Potter and the Forbidden Journey is noted for its ride system, which features seating mounted to robotic arms that move along a track, allowing for synchronization with the complex narrative elements.

Jurassic Park: The Ride
Universal Studios: Hollywood, California (June 21, 1996)

Offering a glimpse of what might have been if John Hammond's prehistoric park from the 1993 feature film had been realized, Jurassic Park: The Ride is Universal's answer to Splash Mountain.

A peaceful outdoor boat ride through Isla Nublar where we marvel at a variety of herbivorous dinosaurs including an Ultrasaurus and Stegosaurus takes an ominous turn as a Parasaurolophus emerges from the lagoon, splashing the boat and turning it off course into the Raptor containment area.

An alarm sounds as we see a marooned motor boat. Though a rescue team has been summoned, we have no choice but to move onward, passing beneath a crate containing a Raptor that jostles about menacingly. Inside the complex, we are slowly brought up an incline as Raptors lunge at the boat. We narrowly escape their reach, only to fall victim to the poisonous venom of a Dilophosaurus waiting in the wings. Finally, coming face to face with a Tyrannous Rex, the boat dives down a waterfall, just as the enormous reptile lunges forward, jaws open wide. We plummet down an eighty-four-foot drop and glide back to the dock to disembark.

The lasting cinematic popularity of *Jurassic Park* and its sequels led to versions of the attraction in Orlando in 1999 and Japan in 2001.

Valhalla

Pleasure Beach: Blackpool, Lancashire, England (June 14, 2000)

We board Viking longboats for a journey into the mythical world beyond the grave for those deemed worthy by the Norse god Odin. Passing through the mouth of a Viking warrior's skull, sound effects and traditional Norse music are heard as we make our way into a dimly lit cavern, where a fearsome, two-headed dog growls as we pass. The ascent up the first lift is lit by two torches, which give off a considerable amount of heat as the boat drifts beneath another guard dog.

The spirit of a Viking warrior warns us of the perils that await, and the music heard throughout the chamber intensifies as the longboat plunges into darkness. Fire, steam, and mythical monsters are seen before we pass through a tunnel for a brief view of the outside world. Suddenly, the boat plummets backwards and turns, taking us into an icy realm of skeleton warriors, and then descending into blackness as it drops sixty feet into a water vortex, passing the wreckage of a Viking ship along the way.

Flickering lights reveal passage through a waterfall and the boat ascends once again into darkness. Two giant logs emerge from the shadows, seemingly on a collision course, but merely create a massive splash.

Torches ignite and the boat dives into a pit of fire, with the brunt of the threat extinguished by the force of its splash. A final scene of a fiery explosion over the skeletal remains of a Viking warrior concludes the ride as the boat sails from the show building and back to the dock where riders disembark, dry off, and can buy a photo of the experience.

A popular attraction, and billed as the world's largest indoor dark ride, Valhalla's mix of impressive effects, dramatic changes in temperature, and water-based thrills is marred slightly by what some consider half-hearted theming.

Voyage to the Iron Reef
Knott's Berry Farm: Buena Park, California (May 15, 2015)

Knott's Berry Farm introduced this interactive 3D dark ride in the spring of 2015.

We board submarine-themed vehicles to wage battle against underwater creatures that have harvested steel from many of the park's most memorable attractions, leaving them in ruins. Armed with blasters built into the ride vehicles, we aim our weapons at screens throughout the attraction, shooting freeze rays at our aquatic enemies until a final showdown with the Kraken Queen.

CHAPTER ELEVEN

Gone into the Gloom

It is rare that Imagineers abandon attraction concepts entirely, but in the sixty-year-plus history of Disney's theme parks, a few ideas have come to naught. Some of these lost attractions owe their fate to the poor box office performance of the films that inspired them, others to the high cost of production and maintenance when reproducing an already existing attraction would prove much easier. Others simply were victims of bad timing or were lost to squabbling between Disney's creative and corporate interests. While by no means comprehensive, the following is a list of some dark rides and associated attractions that were considered at various points in Disney's history.

Disney's Abandoned Dark Ride Concepts

Atlantis Expedition

The box office failure in 2001 of *Atlantis: The Lost Empire* caused a planned re-theming of Tomorrowland's Submarine Voyage to be scrapped. The revamp included a mechanical arm extending from the submarine that guests could use to reach for doubloons and gems scattered on the sea floor.

Baby Herman's Runaway Baby Buggy

Moving forward from an abandoned Epcot pavilion concept celebrating motion pictures, Disney-MGM Studios was originally conceived of as a half-day park. Its initial popularity inspired plans for an area themed to Roger Rabbit's Hollywood, based on the hit 1988 film that mixed animated characters from Disney, Warner Bros., and other animation studios with live actors. In this attraction, guests would find themselves on the set of the Baby Herman cartoon "Tummy Trouble," replacing its temperamental star as they careen through a hospital ward in ride vehicles designed to look like baby buggies. According to Jim Hill Media, this proposed dark ride was "supposed to feature image capture, which means as you exited the ride you'd have the opportunity to buy a picture of you and your friends seated in a giant buggy with all of you wearing baby bonnets."

Benny the Cab

The precursor to what would become Roger Rabbit's Car Toon Spin in Anaheim and Tokyo, Benny the Cab was another attraction planned for a Roger Rabbit-themed area of Disney-MGM Studios in Orlando. Like Baby Herman's Runaway Baby Buggy, due to disputes with Steven Spielberg's Amblin Entertainment over the rights to the characters created for the Roger Rabbit film, these and other related plans were shelved.

The Chinese Theater's Great Disney Movie Villain Ride

A potential 3D adventure and replacement for the Great Movie Ride, where Disney's most iconic villains would have menaced guests before the forces of good finally save the day.

Dick Tracy's Crime Stoppers

In 1990, Disney released a live-action feature film starring Warren Beatty, Al Pacino, Dustin Hoffman, and Madonna under its Touchstone label. The Imagineers planned a companion attraction for both Disney-MGM Studios and a newly conceived Hollywoodland at Disneyland. A promotional press release hinting at what was to come declared:

Guests will literally get "into the act" in this new high-tech action-adventure featuring the very latest in audio-animatronics, simulation, sound and special effects. Guests will join America's favorite comic-strip detective in a high speed chase with his gangster adversaries.

Unfortunately, the movie's box office performance did not meet studio expectations, and the decision was made to cancel plans for this ambitious new EMV dark ride.

Dinorama Meteor Dark Ride

A version of Animal Kingdom's DINOSAUR dark ride aimed at the younger set.

The Enchanted Snow Palace

Planned for Anaheim's Fantasyland, Marc Davis drew extensive concept art for this boat ride on an icy river. As the Northern Lights shone overhead, guests would encounter a wintry world of fairies, snow giants, polar bears, and other scenes of Arctic wildlife, and explore the realm of the Snow Queen.

Enhanced DINOSAUR

Originally, Animal Kingdom's EMV DINOSAUR attraction was intended to feature Ankylosaurus-shaped ride vehicles that took guests on a journey through prehistoric jungles to witness such scenes as volcanic eruptions and a feasting Tyrannosaurus Rex.

The Great Muppet Movie Ride

A parody tour through the history of cinema given as only the Muppets know how, this ride would have been part of a larger Muppet-themed area, along with Muppet*Vision 3D.

Herbie The Love Bug

Planned for Fantasyland in Disneyland sometime around 1976, this dark ride would have taken guests through scenes from the first two Herbie films. As it does in the movie, at the end of the ride the Love Bug would have split in half.

Hotel Mel

Before Twilight Zone Tower of Terror became the wildly popular thrill ride that it is today, Disney-MGM Studios did not have enough attractions to satisfy guest capacity. The Imagineers approached the Hollywood director and writer Mel Brooks about collaborating on a project.

Park guests walking up Sunset Boulevard would encounter a dilapidated old hotel. They would soon find out that Brooks himself is filming his latest movie inside and is looking for extras. Interested guests learn that they have to audition, but are cautioned that the house is rumored to be haunted.

Boarding golf-cart ride vehicles, guests would maneuver through the film set and experience various gags, including a trip through the hotel lobby for an encounter with *The Hunchback of Notre Dame*'s Quasimodo working as a bellman; witches cackling over cauldrons as they prepare dinner in the hotel's kitchen; Dracula, the Wolfman, and the Invisible Man grooming themselves in the men's room; and Frankenstein's monster, realizing he's out of toilet paper, reaching into the next stall, only to find what he thinks is tissue is actually the wrappings of the Mummy.

Clever as many of the gags might have been, the attraction lacked the thrills that park management felt necessary to sustain guest interest, and it was scrapped in favor of the eventual Tower of Terror.

The Incredible Journey Within

Reminiscent of Disneyland's Adventure Thru Inner Space, passengers would travel through replicas of human organs on an overhead ride system much like the one used in Peter Pan's Flight. Though it was deemed too expensive an attraction to maintain considering the set pieces it would require, concepts for the attraction did ultimately inspire Body Wars, which simulated motion through the human body.

Iran Pavilion

When the Shah was overthrown in 1979, plans were abandoned for an Epcot pavilion that would have featured an elaborate dark ride chronicling the history of Persia and its people.

Mary Poppins

Like the Peter Pan's Flight attraction that it nearly replaced in Walt Disney World, guests would float through various scenes, as if guided by Mary Poppins' umbrella. An alternate version employed carousel horses as ride vehicles that would leap in and out of Bert's chalk drawings of different scenes from the film.

Mathmagicland

One of the earliest plans for Anaheim's Tomorrowland featured a dark ride attraction conceived by John Hench, inspired by the Donald Duck short about the importance of math and numbers.

Mickey's Madhouse

Part of a proposed Dumbo's Circusland in the years before Toontown was conceived, Mickey's Madhouse was conceptualized to take place in the early black-and-white era of Mickey Mouse cartoons and was essentially a "wild mouse" roller coaster in a dark ride environment. Imagineer Ward Kimball was involved with the planning of this land, which sadly never came to be.

Micro-World

By the early 1960s, the future had already begun to catch up with Disneyland's Tomorrowland. Walt began looking for ways to revitalize this increasingly outdated section of the park. In the late 1950s, he'd already been considering plans for an extension of the area named Science Land, or Adventures in Science, with an attraction named Micro-World, where guests would be "shrunk" to microscopic size and travel through a drop of water. The distraction of the New York World's Fair and eventually

Walt Disney World would sideline this project, and it would eventually be reborn as Adventure Thru Inner Space.

Monstro the Whale

A shoot-the-chutes attraction planned for Disneyland that fell victim to budget cuts, this Pinocchio-themed attraction, where guests shot out of Monstro's open maw, might have been Disney's first flume ride, if it had been built. Instead, guests had to wait until Splash Mountain was introduced over three decades later.

Moonshine Express

A Disneyland flume ride concept using characters from Country Bear Jamboree that put passengers in a shootout with bad bears who brew moonshine deep in the woods of Bear Country.

The Museum of the Weird

An attraction within an attraction, the Museum of The Weird was conceived by Imagineer Rolly Crump as something of a pre-show for the Haunted Mansion. Employing the many unusual concepts he created, it was cancelled when the attraction shifted from a walk-through to a ride-through to accommodate as many guests as possible, though several of Crump's designs, including the mansion's memorable wallpaper, are now part of the dark ride itself.

Mythia: Land of Legends

A flume ride for a planned area of Disneyland based on the myths of ancient Greece and Rome, some of the attractions for this aborted project would later resurface in plans for the also-canceled Beastly Kingdom.

The Nightmare Before Christmas

After the success of the Tim Burton film, a dark ride was planned featuring characters and themes from *The Nightmare*

Before Christmas. Passengers would board coffin sleighs and relive many of the scenes from the movie, culminating in Jack and Sally's romantic hilltop kiss. Though this attraction never materialized, it would go on to inspire a seasonal overlay of the Haunted Mansion featuring characters from the film, known as Haunted Mansion Holiday in both Anaheim and Tokyo.

Pixie Hollow

Early plans for Walt Disney World's New Fantasyland, first announced in 2009, called for a dark ride themed around Tinker Bell and her fairy friends from the popular series of Pixie Hollow films.

Rainbow Road to Oz

After Walt Disney purchased the rights to many of author L. Frank Baum's classic novels, he began thinking about how best to bring the stories to life. One of the earliest planned additions to Disneyland was Rock Candy Mountain and within this colossal confection would be a dark ride themed around a surprise birthday party for Dorothy in the Emerald City. However, the plans for Rock Candy Mountain were shelved and with it, Rainbow Road to Oz took an extended detour.

The Rhine River Cruise

In this leisurely dark ride, slated for Epcot's Germany Pavilion, guests would cruise down Germany's most famous rivers and enjoy miniature versions of famous landmarks. In *Walt Disney's Epcot Center*, Richard Beard wrote:

> An early concept has guests boarding a "cruise boat" for a simulated ride down the Rhine and other rivers, the trip affording a visual impression in miniature of the cultural heritage of Germany's past and highlights of its present. Among the detailed models envision are scenes in the Black Forest, the Oktoberfest, Heidelberg, the industrial Ruhr Valley... The possibilities are limited only by the planners' imaginations.

Robin Hood

Based on the 1973 animated film, an attempt was made by Imagineer Tony Baxter to translate the character-based feature into a three-dimensional dark ride experience, but plans were soon abandoned. As enjoyable as some may find the film, its forest setting offered little inspiration to the Imagineers when it came time to develop a full-scale attraction.

Sleeping Beauty

A traditional dark ride that might have replaced Snow White's Scary Adventures at Walt Disney World, it featured many of the film's most memorable scenes. Guests would have found themselves on vehicles twisting and turning through the forest of thorns surrounding the castle, confronting Maleficent's ogre goons, and finally facing her dragon form before Prince Phillip and Aurora are reunited.

Spain Pavilion

Another planned expansion of Epcot's World Showcase that did not transpire, this pavilion was to feature a dark ride exploring the culture and people of this vibrant European nation.

The Sword in the Stone

Instead of Mr. Toad's Wild Ride, Walt Disney World may have opened with a dark ride attraction based on the animated feature *The Sword in the Stone*, highlighting its "Wizard's Duel," with guests caught in the middle of the epic battle between Merlin and Madam Mim, but plans fell through.

Thames River Ride

Another river ride that never left port, this one was intended for Epcot's UK pavilion. Guests would sail past Big Ben, the Houses of Parliament, the Tower of London, and other British landmarks.

Voyage Through Time

Conceived for the shelved Discovery Bay project in 1982, this dark ride took inspiration from the stories of H.G. Wells, author of *The Time Machine*. Guests would journey through time to witness scenes from lost civilizations and encounter fantastic creatures both real and mythical. The attraction went through many iterations, including a guided version and flume, before the abandoned time travel concept was later recycled for Animal Kingdom's DINOSAUR.

Western River Expedition

Had demand for Pirates of the Caribbean not been so great when Walt Disney World opened without its own version of the hit Disneyland attraction, this dark ride, a Wild West adventure, might have eventually been the East Coast's answer to the popular boat ride. Done in much the same style as Pirates of the Caribbean, with primary design work done by Marc Davis, the Frontierland attraction would not be realized in Orlando, but elements from Davis' concept work would later inspire the canyon scene in Disneyland Paris' Phantom Manor, itself an update of the Haunted Mansion.

A Future Shrouded In Darkness

Innovation is a moving target and Disney theme parks are constantly being reinvented with new attractions that promise to both engage guests immediately and have a lasting resonance that justifies the time, space, and cost devoted to their creation. As competition among theme parks continues to increase, park guests have become more discerning about the type of attractions available to them and the value created through the experience. Recognizing this, rather than rest on the history of their many notable accomplishments, Disney's Imagineers have continued to embrace the ever-evolving technologies in creating new dark ride attractions.

Though the toolbox of today's Imagineer has expanded exponentially since the days of blacklight paint and the

Pepper's Ghost effect, dark ride design continues to be a "mystical, magnificent hybrid of disciplines," explains Adam Bezark, one-time Imagineer and founder of the Bezark Company, which has contributed to projects for Shanghai Disneyland, Universal Studios' Jurassic Park ride, and Disney's Illuminations and Fantasmic shows.

Many newly developed dark rides, such as Under the Sea ~ Journey of the Little Mermaid and Pirates of the Caribbean: Battle for the Sunken Treasure, have incorporated computer-animated video screens in addition to enhanced audio-animatronics. Others, like Ratatouille: The Adventure, use 3D projection to enhance storytelling, but 3D attractions are not without drawbacks. Phil Bloom, of American Scenic, a California company devoted to theme ride design, said:

> We have used 3D projection in rides as a way of expand-ing the physical environment and to get more dynamic motion from characters than we can get from audio-an-imatronic figures. Though 3D is popular now, 3D glasses are a problem. Handing them out, collecting them, and cleaning them is a hassle and they're annoying to wear.

Dark rides such as Universal Studios' E.T. Adventure and Disneyland's Buzz Lightyear Astro Blasters have long offered park guests a measure of interaction with popular characters, whether it was the chance to hear E.T. thank them by name for helping him return home, or compete against friends and family for bragging rights over who had the fastest gun in Star Command. In 2008, Disney began development of its MyMagic+ system. When they introduced their MagicBands to expedite ticketing, resort access, and the FastPass+ res-ervation system at Disney World in 2013, they hinted at the eventuality of still more benefits from their exploration of the technology and how their latest innovation might manifest in other areas of the park. One would surface in the spring of 2016, when guests wearing MagicBands noticed they received a personalized farewell message when riding "it's a small world" and their names appeared on one of three large screens built into the attraction's final scene. The *Orlando Sentinel*'s Dewayne Bevil wrote:

This surprise and delight moment at 'small world' could be part of a series about which Disney creative types have hinted. For instance, princesses and other characters might be able to address guests by their names without asking through the magic of MagicBands.

The strength, and for some, suspicion, of the MyMagic+ technology is that Disney knows where participating guests are and its implications on the potential to enrich the guest experience are considerable. A young child, celebrating her birthday in Fantasyland, can be surprised by her favorite princess, who greets her by name, instantly creating a memory that lasts a lifetime. Perhaps another guest, touring the newly created Star Wars Land, is suddenly taken prisoner by the First Order on suspicion that he sympathizes with the Resistance.

As advancing technologies allow Disney's Imagineers to introduce new opportunities for interactive experiences, we should expect that these personal touches become a more standard part of story immersion on dark rides and throughout Disney theme parks. How Imagineers use technology to revitalize the storytelling medium and world building in the very near future may be just the sort of thing Walt Disney once envisioned for Tomorrowland and his unrealized dream of Epcot.

In fact, during the 2017 South By Southwest Film Festival, an annual event held in Austin, Texas, representatives from Disney's research and development division were on hand to showcase just how close they are to introducing the next generation of guest immersion. Jon Snoddy, senior vice president for research and development, brought to light how artificial intelligence and storytelling robots would offer an unprecedented degree of guest interaction with the fantasy worlds created by park designers. Suggesting the potential of "things like characters that can move around among our guests," he offered video of a robotic Pascal, Rapunzel's lizard sidekick from 2010's *Tangled*, but noted that before such creations are unleashed in the parks, "they're going to need to understand where they're going, have goals, and they're going to have to know how to navigate in a world with humans." And like those before him in the ranks of Disney's roster of creative men and women who have embraced this continued modernization, Snoddy makes it clear that for the current crop of Imagineers technology continues to takes a back seat to story and engagement:

> We're not going to put up a sign that says "Look! Artificial Intelligence," because no one would come to see that. They really come to be moved emotionally. That will not change.

One intriguing innovation that Disney has yet to explore in its parks is the potential of Oculus Rift. Initially developed in 2012, the technology allows for the complete immersion in three-dimensional worlds through a virtual reality headset. A simulated environment is created that users can then navigate and interact with, depending on the technology at hand. Imagine skydiving, scuba diving, or even setting sail aboard the *Jolly Roger* from the comfort of your chair. Though they have announced a partnership with the creator of the technology to develop film and other material, what might be the potential of this medium when applied to the theme park environment? A reimagined entertainment complex in the vein of the now-closed DisneyQuest? Long-shuttered dark rides reborn to be experienced by new generations in the virtual realm? If we can dream it, perhaps *they* can do it?

How these and other pioneering methods of theme park entertainment manifest in Disney's dark rides in the years to come as the technology matures is anyone's guess, but the few attractions on the immediate horizon suggest that the Imagineers fortunately have not lost sight of the core element of narrative immersion. These upcoming Disney dark rides will each employ technologies old and new to draw guests into the world created by the Imagineers, but like the vehicle chosen or a specific effect, is ultimately only a tool in service to the story being told. As former head of Imagineering Marty Sklar once noted:

In a Disney park, not only is storytelling "the thing"—every thing tells a story.

Ant-Man Ride

Opening Date: 2018

A re-theming of Buzz Lightyear's Astro Blasters in Hong Kong Disneyland to coincide with the 2018 release of the Marvel film *Ant-Man and the Wasp*. Part of a $1.4 billion multi-year expansion project, set to conclude in 2023, the attraction will be Hong Kong Disneyland's second Marvel-based attraction, following the debut of the Iron Man Experience, a 3D motion simulator that opened in early 2017.

First Order Ride

Opening Date: 2019

Still largely the subject of speculation, Disney's construction of Star Wars-themed lands in its Anaheim and Orlando parks has nonetheless generated considerable interest among park goers and fans of the forty-year-old film franchise in advance of the area's announced 2019 opening. According to Ken Storey in *Orlando Weekly,* one of the two new attractions is rumored to be an interactive dark ride featuring one-hundred-and-fifty audio-animatronic Stormtroopers:

> Thrust into the middle of a battle between the First Order and the Resistance, passengers will board track-less vehicles and at a certain point during the experience, disembark the vehicle to proceed through an interactive environment on foot, before reboarding and continuing the ride.

As hinted at by designs previewed at 2017's D23 Expo, guests are expected to maneuver through a massive First Order ship aboard transport vehicles guided by astro-mech droids programmed with ship schematics and security codes.

Beauty and the Beast Ride

Opening Date: Spring 2020

A 2016 press release by the Oriental Land Company, Disney's licensing partner for the Tokyo theme parks, revealed plans for a new, as-yet-unnamed dark ride adventure through the Beast's

Castle, "where guests ride enchanted serving dishes" that dance to the film's beloved songs. Guests follow Belle through a musical adventure as she warms the cold heart of the Beast and breaks the spell on the castle and all who live there. This trackless ride is expected to last approximately eight minutes.

Mickey and Minnie's Runaway Railway
Opening Date: TBD

Taking the place of the iconic Great Movie Ride in Disney's Hollywood Studios, Mickey and Minnie's Runaway Railway, for the first time, gives Disney's most iconic character a starring role in his own attraction, as guests step through a movie screen into a world inspired by the classic shorts to join Mickey, Minnie, and friends for a thrilling adventure through an innovative screen-based dark ride, as Mickey and Minnie plan a picnic together. With its style based on the current look of Mickey Mouse cartoons, the attraction will feature a new theme song and the largest amount of hidden Mickeys in any ride, yet.

Ratatouille: The Adventure
Opening Date: TBD

Similar to the trackless ride experience at Walt Disney Studios in Paris, this ride was announced for inclusion in Epcot's France Pavilion.

Epilogue

Time and again throughout this text, the point has been raised that a dark ride takes its name not from the absence, but the careful manipulation of light, and that the best of these attractions (exemplified by those first introduced in Disneyland decades ago) set the standard through their use of theming and sets, music, audio, and visual effects, to transport users to a different time or place.

We began with a discussion of the nature of fear and our attraction to it. Why do people enjoy experiences—whether they are books, films, or theme park attractions—which sometimes evoke negative or even terrifying emotions? Looking back even further than Charles Darwin, there are some who suggest that the Greek philosopher Aristotle felt the people of his day were so enamored with dramatic tragedy because the spectacle of painful events allowed for a catharsis—the feelings of fear and pity experienced by an audience were therapeutic, even pleasurable, in that they resulted in a cleansing of the emotional palate. While Disney's earliest dark rides often simply applied familiar Disney characters and scenes to ride technologies that had already been in use for some time, even at their earliest, they offered the innovation of establishing a connection with their guests through the stories they were telling. In many ways, classic attractions like Peter Pan's Flight and Mr. Toad's Wild Ride remain as popular today as the animated films that inspired them.

From its inception, the notion of the Disney dark ride has implied a careful balance of scenic elements mixed with technology, sound, and effects, all carefully manipulated in service to the story being conveyed. The best of them have always revealed precious little of the secrets in their design, hoping instead that guests would be convinced by the spectacle that they have temporarily escaped mundane reality for this alternate world of fantasy.

As the years passed and Imagineers raised the bar to create guest experiences that were not based on already familiar properties, the innovations continued in both storytelling and ride design, with attractions like Haunted Mansion and Pirates of the Caribbean, and later still with new entries such as Pooh's Hunny Hunt, Mystic Manor, Monsters, Inc. Ride & Go Seek!, and Ratatouille: The Adventure.

Core to the success of these attractions and countless others like them has been Disney's commitment to an immersive design—creating new and separate realities and inviting guests to experience them. Just as moviegoers are meant to suspend disbelief when the lights of a theater dim and the opening credits fade to reveal their favorite stars on the big screen, the narrative structure of the dark ride allows the same experience in the theme park environment. Of vital import to the ongoing popularity of these attractions is the extent of the immersion. As was the case in the plays considered by Aristotle, if guests become emotionally detached when experiencing a dark ride, they become removed from it. If something in the world they have been inserted into feels artificial, it becomes easy to be pulled out of the narrative and the illusion of life is destroyed along with the opportunity to establish that all-important connection.

Entering Discoveryland in Disneyland Paris or Treasure Cove in Shanghai, we become part of the spectacle as designers intended, and the more believable the environment the Imagineers have created, the more emotionally engaged we become as guests. Will it delight our children? Does it renew a spark of a long-ago memory of our own? With Disney's films serving as the inspiration for so many of their most iconic dark rides, this feeling of engagement can become even more powerful when we as guests become the protagonist in the attraction. Rather than reacting to the screen image of Snow White's shock and terror as she flees through the forest, we *become* her, witnessing those same dreadful scenes, and like Pinocchio, *we* narrowly escape the jaws of the menacing Monstro. And when preparing to sail into dark and dangerous waters, *we* are warned to "keep a weather eye open" and steel ourselves for the perils awaiting *us* courtesy of Pirates of the Caribbean.

Whereas the films and ideas that have inspired Disney's classic animated features have so long resonated due to their well-written stories, beautiful animation, and compelling characters, in the dark ride environment, passengers are made part of the story and are no longer simply passive observers. When everything works as the designers have intended, the combination of technology, effects, world building, interactivity, and narrative connects with us on an emotional level that can be as engaging as any film and as thrilling as any roller coaster. Our joy, our panic, our fear, and our relief are let loose, all within the confines of a four-minute experience.

In the best of these attractions, we—the park goers— become both the heart and the darkness.

Bibliography

Adams, Judith A. *The American Amusement Park Industry*. 1st ed. Boston: Twayne Publishers, 1991. Print.

Alcorn, Steve. *Theme Park Design*. 1st ed. Orlando: Theme Perks, Inc., 2010. Print.

Baham, Jeff. *An Unofficial History of Disney's Haunted Mansion*. 1st ed. Doombuggies.com, 2010. Print.

Bailyn, Sasha. "Shining a Light on Dark Rides." Entertainment Designer. Web. Accessed 20 February 2017.

Balogh, Chris. "12 Proposed Disney Attractions That Were Never Built." MentalFloss.com. Web. Accessed 13 February 2017

"The Bill Tracy Project." BillTracyProject.com. Web. Accessed 12 Mar. 2017.

Beeton, Sue. *Travel, Tourism and the Moving Image*. 1st ed. Bristol, UK: Channel View Publications, 2015. Print.

Benson, Carl Frederick and Taylor Littleton. *The Idea of Tragedy*. 1st ed. Scott, Foresman, 1966. Print.

Bevil, Dewayne. "Disney: 'Small World' Says Goodbye to You and Your Magicband." OrlandoSentinel.com. Web. Accessed 14 March. 2017.

Brahic, Catherine. "Prehistoric Cinema: A Silver Screen on the Cave Wall." *New Scientist*. Web. Accessed 15 September 2016.

Carr, Austin. "The Messy Business Of Reinventing Happiness: Inside Disney's Radical Plan to Modernize Its Cherished Theme Parks." FastCompany.com. Web. 15 Accessed 23 February 2017.

Carnahan, Alyssa. "Look Closer: 1964 New York World's Fair." The Walt Disney Family Museum. Web. Accessed 22 Feb. 2017.

Cohen, Roger. "Euro Disney Encounters Real World." OrlandoSentinel.com. Web. Accessed 8 March 2017.

Coons, Sam. "The Historical Development of Themed Space: The History of the Dark Ride." Theoryofthemeparks.blogspot. com. Web. Accessed 9 September 2016.

Creighton, Elizabeth. "Tale as Old as Time: Storytelling and the Art of Dark Ride Design." Scholarcommons.sc.edu. Web. Accessed 21 Sept. 2016.

Crump, Rolly. *It's Kind of a Cute Story*. Bamboo Forest Publishing, 2012. Print.

Darwin, Charles. *The Expression of the Emotions in Man and Animals*. 1st ed. Oxford University Press, 2009. Print.

Davision. "The History of the Roller Coaster." Davison.com. N.p., 2017. Web. Accessed 22 Sept. 2016.

Dingles Fairground Heritage Centre. "Dark Rides." Dingles Fairground Heritage Centre. Accessed 10 October 2016.

Disney Book Group. *Marc Davis: Walt Disney's Renaissance Man*. Disney Editions, 2014. Print.

Disney Extinct Attractions. "Disney Extinct Attractions: Adventure Thru Inner Space." Disney Extinct Attractions. Web. Accessed 19 January 2017.

Disney Wiki. "Disney Wiki." Disney.wikia.com. Web. Accessed 3 October 2016.

Dixon, Jeff. "A Walt Disney Ride That Never Was." Keytothekingdombook.com. Web. Accessed 2 March 2017.

Doombuggies.com "Welcome, Foolish Mortals... To Doombuggies—A Tribute to Disney's Haunted Mansion." Doombuggies.com. Web. 13 February 2017.

Entertainment Designer.com. "Laughter In The Dark: A History Of Dark Rides—Entertainment Designer." Entertainment Designer. Web. Accessed 21 September 2016.

ExtinctDisney.com "Extinct Disney." ExtinctDisney. Web. Accessed 10 January 2017.

Frontierland Station. "What You Don't Know About Disneyland's Pirates of the Caribbean." *Frontierland Station.* 2017. Web. Accessed 25 January 2017.

Gabler, Neal. Walt Disney: *The Triumph of the American Imagination.* Alfred A. Knopf, 2006. Print.

Gayle, Damien. Gayle, Damien. "A Night at the Pictures, Caveman Style.'" Mail Online. Web. Accessed 10 September 2016.

Gordon, Bruce et al. *Disneyland: The Nickel Tour.* 1st ed. Santa Clara, Calif.: Camphor Tree Publishers, 1995. Print.

Grassi, Ralph. "Welcome to Funchase Jungleland." Funchase. com. Accessed 13 March 2017.

Grubb, Jeff. "Disney Is Coming to Oculus Rift." VentureBeat. Web. Accessed 21 February 2017.

Hahner, David. "Ghost Ship." Dafe.org. Web. Accessed 13 March 2017.

Harbourn, Jennifer. "5 Disneyland Rides That Were Never Built." Theme Park Tourist. Web. Accessed 22 February 2017.

Hench, John et al. *Designing Disney.* 1st ed. New York: Disney Editions, 2008. Print.

Hill, Jim. "Why For?—Hotel Mel, Where's My Mummy, and Who Broke Tik Tok?" JimHillMedia.com. Web. Accessed 4 February 2017.

Hunter, Honor. "The Disney Lands That Time Forgot..." Blueskydisney.com. Web. Accessed 15 February 2017.

ImagineeringDisney.com. "Rhine River Cruise Mysteries." Imagineeringdisney.com. Web. 22 February 2017.

The Imagineers, with Lefkon, Wendy. *Walt Disney Imagineering: A Behind the Scenes Look at Making Magic Real.* Disney Editions, 1996. Print.

The Imagineers, with Malmberg, Melody. *Walt Disney Imagineering: A Behind the Scenes Look at Making MORE Magic Real.* Disney Editions, 2010. Print.

KingdomofMemories.com. Mickey's Madhouse." Kingdomofmemories.com. PDF File. 5 March 2017.

Korkis, Jim. *The Revised Vault of Walt*. Theme Park Press, 2012. Print.

Korkis, Jim. "WDW Chronicles—Year One: The WDW That Almost Was." Allears.net. Web. Accessed 20 February 2017.

Krosnick, Brian. "BODY WARS: The "Inside Story of the Lost Epcot E-Ticket That Left Riders Queasy." Theme Park Tourist. Web. Accessed 23 February 2017.

Kurtti, Jeff with Gordon, Bruce. *The Art of Disneyland*. Disney Editions, 2006. Print.

Kurtti, Jeff. *Walt Disney's Imagineering Legends and the Genesis of the Disney Theme Park*. Disney Editions, 2008. Print.

Kurrti, Jeff and Gordon, Bruce. *The Art of Walt Disney World Resort*. Disney Editions, 2009. Print.

Kwaitek, Brandon. "The Dark Ride." Digitalcommons.wku.edu. Web. Accessed 22 September 2016.

Lawrence, Daz. "A Short History of Ghost Train Rides." HORRORPEDIA. Web. Accessed 23 September 2016.

Laister, Nick. "Dark Rides." Dingles Fairground Heritage Centre. Accessed 22 September 2016.

Lee, Banks. "Hong Kong Disneyland to Get Transformed Castle, New Marvel Area, and More." Attractions Magazine. Web. Accessed 4 March 2017.

Lee, Dave. "SXSW 2017: Disney 'Not in the Business of Scaring Kids!'" BBC News. Web. Accessed 14 March 2017.

Littaye, Alain. "A Disney-MGM Studios Celebration—Part Four—The Dick Tracy Crime Stoppers Attraction That Never Was—Original Artwork." Disneyandmore.blogspot.com. Web. Accessed 24 February 2017.

Lovecraft, Howard Phillips. *Supernatural Horror in Literature*. Dover Publications, 2012. Print.

Luca, Bill. "Send 'Em Out Laffing—The Pretzel Amusement Ride Co. P.1." Laffinthedark.com. Web. Accessed 22 Sept. 2016.

Lukas, Scott A. *Theme Park*. Reaktion Books, 2008. Print.

Lucas, F.L.. *Tragedy in Relation to Aristotle's Poetics*. Harcourt, Brace. 1928.

Lumeneck, Lou. "'Tomorrowland,' Disney and Their Links to The 1964-65 World's Fair." *New York Post*. Web. Accessed 22 February 2017.

Mangels, William F. *The Outdoor Amusement Industry: From the Earliest Times to the Present*. Vantage Press, 1952. Print.

MacDonald, MacDonald, Brady. "25 Best Theme Park Dark Rides In The World." *Los Angeles Times*. Web. Accessed 13 March 2017.

Miller, Ron. "In 1951, You Could Pay 50 Cents to Ride an Airship to the Moon." Gizmodo.com Web. Accessed 22 September 2016.

Notaro, Joe. "Disney Stuck on the Drawing Board: Maroon Studios & Roger Rabbit's Hollywood—WDW News Today." WDW News Today. Web. Accessed 2 February 2017.

Oriental Land Company "Press Release." http://www.olc.co.jp/en/news/olcgroup/20160427_01e.pdf. Web. Accessed 7 March 2017.

Perry, Nick. "Arrow Development—A Forgotten Piece of Mountain View's Past. (July 26, 2002)." Mv-voice.com. Accessed 13 January 2017.

Poblete, Jordan. "China's Relationship with the Walt Disney Company Is a Diplomatic One Just As Much It Is a Business One." DisneyExaminer. Web. 11 March 2017.

Project Gutenberg. "List Of Never Built Walt Disney World Attractions." Self.gutenberg.org. Web. Accessed 24 Feb. 2017.

Ravenswood-Manor.com "Ravenswood Manor—A Tribute to Thunder Mesa at Disneyland Paris." Ravenswood-manor.com. Web. Accessed 19 February 2017.

Register, Woody. *The Kid of Coney Island: Fred Thompson and the Rise of American Amusements*. Oxford University Press, 2001. Print.

Ridemad.com "Early Dark Ride History in a Nutshell. Ridemad. com. Web. Accessed 21 September 2016.

Riding, Alan. "Only the French Elite Scorn Mickey's Debut." *The New York Times*. Web. Accessed 8 March 2017.

Samuelson, Dale and Yegoiants, Wendy. *The American Amusement Park*. MBI Publishing Company, 2001. Print.

The Science Of Disney Imagineering. Design and Models. Elk Grove, IL: Disney Educational Productions, 2009. DVD.

Sanchez, Andrea. "Here's What Some Imagineers Do After They Leave Disney." DisneyExaminer. Web. Accessed 26 Feb. 2017.

Schmidt, Chuck. "Setting the Record Straight on Disney's Omnimover System." SILive.com. Web. Accesssed 13 Jan. 2017.

Silvester. William. *Building Magic: Disney's Overseas Theme Parks*. 2016. Print.

Sklar, Martin. *Dream It! Do It! My Half-Century Creating Disney's Magic Kingdoms*. Disney Editions, 2013. Print.

Stanton, Jeffrey. "Early Roller Coasters—1870—1886 Lamarcus Thompson Did NOT Invent or Build the First Roller Coaster In America.." Westland.net. Web. Accessed 22 September 2016.

Storey, Ken. "Disney's New Star Wars Ride May Kick Guests Off And Make Them Walk Partway." *Orlando Weekly*. Web. Accessed 22 February 2017.

Studiocentral.com "History of Toy Story Midway Mania." Studioscentral.com. Web. Accessed 13 January, 2017.

Stuprich, Michael. *Horror. The Greenhaven Press Companion to Literary Movements and Genres*. Greenhaven Press, 2001. Print.

Sumner, Mark W. Amusement Park Ride with Underwater-Controlled Boats. U.S. Patent 8,091,483 B1 filed March 31, 2011 and issued January 10, 2012. Print.

Surrell, Jason. *The Haunted Mansion: Imagineering a Disney Classic*. Disney Editions, 2015. Print.

Surrell, Jason. *Pirates of the Caribbean: From the Magic Kingdom to the Movies*. Disney Editions, 2005. Print.

Thomas, Bob. *Walt Disney: An American Original*. Pocket Books, 1976. Print.

Trimborn, Harry. "From the Archives: Wizard of Fantasy Walt Disney Dies." *Los Angeles Times*. Web. Accessed 25 January 2017.

Vaughn, Vicki. "Culture Shock at Euro Disney Park's Challenge: French Don't Snack, Europeans Treat Dogs Like Royalty." tribunedigital-orlandosentinel. Web. Accessed 8 March 2017.

Viszoki, Christy. "The World That Never Was: Nightmare Before Christmas—WDW Radio." WDW Radio. Web. Accessed 6 March. 2017.

Walt Disney World for Grownups. "Rides That Never Were: Walt Disney World—Western River Expedition." Wdwforgrownups. com. Web. 7 February 2017.

Walt Disney Home Entertainment. *Walt Disney Treasures— Disneyland—Secrets, Stories & Magic. Disneyland Goes to the World's Fair*. Buena Vista Home Entertainment, 2007. DVD.

Walt Disney Home Entertainment. *Walt Disney Treasures— Tomorrow Land: Disney in Space and Beyond. EPCOT TV Special*. Buena Vista Home Entertainment, 2004. DVD.

WED Enterprises. Disneyland Original Prospectus 1953." Archive.org. Web. Accessed 23 September 2016.

Weisenberger, Nick. "Secrets Behind Shanghai Disneyland's Pirates of the Caribbean." Coaster 101. Web. Accessed 30 January 2017.

Wright, Alex. *The Imagineering Field Guide to Disneyland*. 1st ed. Print. Disney Editions, 2008. Print.

Yokota, Masao. *Japanese Animation: East Asian Perspectives*. University Press of Mississippi, 2013. Print.

Younger, David. *Theme Park Design & the Art of Themed Entertainment*. Inklingwood Press, 2016. Print.

Zika, Joel. "The Dawn of the Dark Ride at the Amusement Park." Academia.edu. Web. Accessed 23 September 2016.

Zorich, Zach. "Early Humans Made Animated Art—Issue 11: Light—Nautilus." Nautilus. Web. Accessed 22 September 2016.

About the Author

Though I would not begin writing this book until the fall of 2016, its genesis dates back to the first time I watched Disney's *Peter Pan* as a young boy and dreamed that I, too, could one day take flight to Neverland, a feeling shared by countless others since the film's 1953 debut.

A native of Buffalo, New York, it was not until I was in my late twenties that I visited a Disney theme park. During the iconic dark ride's 40th anniversary celebration, cranky spirits would interrupt my first-ever ride through the Haunted Mansion, when a 5.2 magnitude earthquake rocked southern California and passengers were escorted through the length of the attraction with the lights turned on, to the comparative safety of New Orleans Square.

Since that day when the curtain was pulled back, revealing so much of the magic, I have been a frequent visitor to Disney's resorts, along with other theme parks around the world, delighting in the sense of wonder, escapism, and innovation offered by the dark ride genre.

ABOUT THEME PARK PRESS

Theme Park Press publishes books primarily about the Disney company, its history, culture, films, animation, and theme parks, as well as theme parks in general.

Our authors include noted historians, animators, Imagineers, and experts in the theme park industry.

We also publish many books by first-time authors, with topics ranging from fiction to theme park guides.

And we're always looking for new talent. If you'd like to write for us, or if you're interested in the many other titles in our catalog, please visit:

www.ThemeParkPress.com

• •

Theme Park Press Newsletter

Subscribe to our free email newsletter and enjoy:

- ◆ Free book downloads and giveaways
- ◆ Access to excerpts from our many books
- ◆ Announcements of forthcoming releases
- ◆ Exclusive additional content and chapters
- ◆ And more good stuff available nowhere else

To subscribe, visit www.ThemeParkPress.com, or send email to newsletter@themeparkpress.com.

Read more about these books
and our many other titles at:

www.ThemeParkPress.com

Made in the USA
Columbia, SC
11 January 2018